Howl for Now

Editor: Simon Warner

route

First Published in 2005 by Route
PO Box 167, Pontefract, WF8 4WW, UK
e-mail: info@route-online.com
web: www.route-online.com

ISBN: 1 901927 25 3

Editor:
Simon Warner

Cover Illustration:
Michael Anderson

Cover Design:
Andy Campbell
www.absolutely-nothing.com

Support:
Isabel Galán, Ian Daley, Anthony Cropper

Printed by Bookmarque, Croydon

A catalogue for this book is available from the British Library

Route is an imprint of ID Publishing
www.id-publishing.com

Contents

Howl for Now
Preface

Simon Warner

Howl for Now is a volume published in conjunction with a performance of the same name, staged on October 7th, 2005, in the Clothworkers' Centenary Concert Hall in the School of Music of the University of Leeds in the UK. Like the performance, the volume commemorates the 50th anniversary of Allen Ginsberg's first reading of his epic protest poem 'Howl' in the Six Gallery in San Francisco on October 7th, 1955.

The performance incorporated spoken word, dramatic dialogue, visual imagery and a series of newly commissioned musical works responding to the original Ginsberg work. The book aims to reflect something of the diversity of the show, its multi-disciplinary nature, by gathering a body of articles which touch upon a number of aspects of 'Howl' the poem: how its enduring power provides an ongoing inspiration for work by artists and academics, by those making music or working in theatre, by those involved in the visual arts and film-making.

The book *Howl for Now* gathers writers and practitioners from both sides of the Atlantic, including individuals who were personally associated with Allen Ginsberg. David Meltzer, who pens the foreword, has spent more than half a century as poet, novelist, musician and commentator, involved first with the original Beat influx in the Bay Area of the mid-1950s then subsequently participating in and charting an important moment in literary history now generally regarded as the wider San Francisco Poetry Renaissance.

Steven Taylor, who contributes the introduction, is a British-born musician and academic, who moved to the US in the mid-1960s. For the last twenty years of Ginsberg's life – the poet died in 1997 – Taylor was his guitar accompanist at hundreds of performances. He is now Associate Professor at the Jack Kerouac School of Disembodied Poetics at Naropa University in Boulder, Colorado.

The articles that follow emerge from a number of sources. Most have been produced by academics, engaged in a range of disciplines, at the University of Leeds who were directly involved with the *Howl for Now* performance, and who approach, in this collection, matters of text and context, practice and theory, from several perspectives.

Theatre director George Rodosthenous examines the dramatic power of 'Howl''s language. Composer Michael Spencer provides an account of the ways in which he and other invited composers approached the problem of a musical response to Ginsberg's text. Painter Michael Anderson reflects on how 'Howl', in its time and place, connected with developments in the period in the visual arts. My own piece contemplates the political, social and artistic setting into which 'Howl' stepped in the heart of Fifties America.

The remaining items have a speculative quality to them – interviews with the American film-maker Ronald Nameth and the British rock musician Bill Nelson. Both intend to work on a film project with 'Howl' at its centre. Nameth, based today in Sweden, is best known for his celebrated 1966 documentary *Andy Warhol's Exploding Plastic Inevitable*. Nelson, who will provide a soundtrack, is best known for his work with the bands Be Bop Deluxe and Red Noise. Their comments and responses describe what the Beat ethos has meant to them as artists and reveal how Ginsberg's 'Howl', and the wider literature that arose from that community of ground-breaking novelists and poets, can provide a contemporary springboard for the film director and the film composer in the early years of the 21st Century.

The book has at least two intentions – it is a commemoration of an influential work of literature on a significant anniversary and it is also an attempt to pay tribute to 'Howl''s continuing resonance, fifty years after its premiere. We hope that the performance and this volume have played a small part in drawing attention to that continuum. The poem speaks, of course, for itself, half a century after its historic unveiling; *Howl for Now* hopes to remind readers, old and new, that if Ginsberg's piece opens a window on the past it also has the ability to cast light on the present.

Simon Warner
Editor

Credits and acknowledgements

Howl for Now, the performance, was presented in association with the School of Music, the University of Leeds, PopuLUs, the Centre for the Study of the World's Popular Musics and *Chapter & Verse, A Journal of Popular Music and Literature Studies* (www.popmatters.com/ chapter). We would like to thank the directors, composers and musicians who played a part in this presentation, and members of the School for their assistance.

Howl for Now, the book, acknowledges the input of all its contributors. Credit is also due to the publisher, Ian Daley of Route, whose consistent support for this project has been an essential ingredient.

Howling wolves
Foreword

David Meltzer

A displaced person from Brooklyn in Fifties Hollywood mañana culture of bus stop benches with funeral home and supermarket adverts splashed on the wood where we non-drivers sat waiting for the trolleys to pick us up and take us either downtown to the train station to escape or down to the ocean into the Fun Zone.

The first City Lights books were available at the outdoor newsstand on Highland Avenue off Hollywood Boulevard. That's where I read 'Howl' without buying it because I couldn't afford it. (Was a sad sack booster & unable to consider slipping it into my jeans back pocket.)

What I knew was the underground energies of the NYC culture I'd been exiled from. I was a bebop baby, 11 years-old, going either with my father or alone to Birdland and Bop City to sit in the peanut gallery and dig Bird, Monk, Miles, Bud Powell, Max Roach, Mingus. Really dug it. Bebop was 'my music' in the same way that, let's say, 'punk' was in its breakthrough and ultimate containment.

Everything about 'Howl' made sense to this shallow callow 18 year-old exile. The hipster subculture, NYC, the resistant Jewish cadences infused with Blake but really Whitman, the great modernist maestro of the urban vaudeville.

Fast cut to 1957. Twenty year-old David migrates to San Francisco. Takes a bargain flight with artist Wallace Berman – he's spending the weekend, I'm going to stay and work at Paper Editions, a paperback wholesale warehouse.

Wallace and I take turns going to the bathroom with a round

window to turn-on. There's a full moon. I dig it. We're picked up by Elias (godfather of the light shows) and Idell Romero (mystic poet) and taken to their Potrero Hill pad, smoking the local weed as we wend through the night-time streets.

Start hanging out at City Lights. The implacable presence behind the counter is Shig Mauro. Meet Lawrence Ferlinghetti, whose *Pictures of The Gone World* I also read, for free, at the Highland Avenue news-stand.

Got involved with the local poetry scene with peers like Michael McClure, Lew Welch, Joanne Kyger, Lenore Kandel, Philip Whalen, Jack Spicer, Robert Duncan, roll credits.

First met Allen when he and Peter Orlovsky were en route from Europe to the Journey to the East. Allen brought an immediate excitement and energy to everything. As the decades unrolled, I was convinced that Allen knew everybody and everybody knew Allen.

The power of 'Howl' was its roar of hope despite the post-war despair, it was a prophetic gesture in the sense that Blake's 'Jerusalem' was. It summed up, as it critiqued, the historical moment. More than that, it took poetry out of its captivity in the laboratories of universities.

Like Whitman, Allen returned the possibility of poetry back to a democratic constituency. He and his comrades made poetry exciting, egalitarian public events and inspired new generations of poetry.

The poem and I are fifty
Introduction

Steven Taylor

You have to be inspired to write something like that …
You have to have the right historical situation, the right
physical combination, the right mental formation, the
right courage, the right sense of prophecy, and the right
information.

(Schumacher, 1992, p207)

When I met Allen Ginsberg, he was fifty years old; I was twenty-one, and so was 'Howl'. Now the poem and I are fifty, and the poet has been gone near a decade. We worked together for twenty years. At the outset, we promised to tell each other all our secrets. He was big on vows; 'who fell on their knees in hopeless cathedrals praying for each other's salvation and light and breasts, until the soul illuminated its hair for a second' (Miles, 1986, p5). He used to tell people that I taught him music and he taught me poetry. There's some truth to this, but I got the better part of the bargain. I came of age in his company.

We were well matched musically from the moment I joined him on stage at my college to improvise an accompaniment to his songs. We liked the same things, Beethoven, brass bands, old ballads, the blues and all that proceeded from it, and singing. Singing was our great pleasure. He had the basso and I the high baritone. Some serious types didn't like his singing, but he was in tune, on time, and fearless about it. He could harmonize, make the changes, and not get lost. 'Solid,' he would say. In performance, he

17

was solid, committed, all there. There was a peculiar elegance to his delivery and, when he went ecstatic, he was as true as the best of them.

Early on it struck me that although Allen was older than my father, he spoke as I did. His cohort had bequeathed the language that my generation assumed it had invented. 'Howl' was part of a broad, mid-century democratisation that links the Montgomery bus boycott and the people stopping a war in South East Asia with a president's wife shaking her money-maker at the Electric Circus. That the most widely known poem of the 20th Century had its premier in a converted garage was a signal instance in a larger trend.

One major thread running through this 'democratisation' (Ginsberg's term) was African-American music. US culture's (and counterculture's) debt to African America will never be adequately expressed. For present purposes, I'll note that jazz was mainstream popular music during Ginsberg's formative years, and that all his life he studied the blues. 'Howl''s opening riff, 'I saw the best minds of my generation' might be conventionally described as two dactyls and a trochee, but could also be heard as a measure of 12/8 blues. Allen tended to favour compound meter, like 12/8, because it swings. There's a recording of Elvin Jones drumming along with his reading of a later poem, 'Hum Bomb'. They were a natural match. I think of 'Howl' as a saxophone solo – 'and rose reincarnate in the ghostly clothes of jazz in the goldhorn shadow of the band and blew the suffering of America's naked mind into an eli eli lamma lamma sabacthani saxophone cry that shivered the cities down to the last radio' (Miles, 1986, p6). It takes a tenor-man's lungs to blow it.

Ginsberg never said that 'Howl' is a sax solo. I think of it that way because the metaphor comes up a lot in Beat writing. Kerouac referred to his *Mexico City Blues* poems as a series of 242 improvised saxophone choruses, and at the start of 'Kaddish', Part 2, Allen portrays his mother Naomi's 'history' as 'a few images/run thru the mind–like the saxophone chorus of houses and years'. Allen told me that jazz was black speech, and he described his poetics as 'bop prosody'. The Beats' language was, rhythmically at least, indebted to 1940s Harlem jive. From reading 'Howl' aloud, I get the impression of a virtuoso piece requiring a wind player's lungs.

Allen's father, Louis Ginsberg, was a teacher of English literature and respected lyric poet. At seventeen, in 1943, Allen was accepted into a university with a first-rate English department. During his second term, he met Lucien Carr, with whom he read the French symbolists, and who introduced him to Jack Kerouac and William Burroughs; together they concocted a 'New Vision' based on Rimbaud's idea of the poet as seer. In 1950, at 24, Ginsberg introduced himself to William Carlos Williams, who became a friend and mentor. Allen also connected with Charles Reznikoff who for decades, beginning in the 19-teens, walked around NYC noting anecdotal poems where events in the lives of ordinary people take on cosmic resonance. In this sense, Ginsberg is closer to Reznikoff than to Williams.

Allen was a city boy, born in Newark, raised in Paterson, schooled in New York, premiered in San Francisco, went native in Benares, played the capitals of Europe, retired to a teaching post in Brooklyn, died on the Lower East Side. He spent most of his life in the sort of downtown tenements that had housed his mother after she fled the pogrom. Ginsberg was the rare 20th Century American male who had never driven a car. All his life, he walked around cities with companions; 'who talked continuously seventy two hours from park to pad to bar to Bellevue to museum to the

Brooklyn Bridge' (Miles, 1986, p3). His work came of this.

Loneliness figures also. 'Howl' is full of loss, abandonment, and solitude, friends who jumped from tenement roofs, fell out of subway windows, or 'vanished into nowhere Zen New Jersey', (Miles, 1986, p3) but these losses echo a larger one. 'Howl' is a prelude to 'Kaddish' in more than a chronological sense. Beneath 'Howl' is the protracted process of losing his mother. Naomi didn't die until Allen was thirty (the year 'Howl' was published), but she began her spectacular exit when he was a child. I had the impression that he felt himself very much alone. There's a passage in 'Howl' that speaks to this. On a good night, he'd let it loose in a weeping roar: 'Moloch in whom I sit lonely! [breathe] Moloch in whom I dream angels! [breathe, wipe your nose] Crazy in Moloch! [breathe] Cock *sucker* in Moloch! [breathe, go fortississimo] *Lack*love and *man*less in Moloch!' (Miles, 1986, p6).

'Howl' is about family, friends, lovers, nations that go mad, or die, or try to. Mother checked out, and so will everyone else. (It's hard to be with someone who assumes that you are about to go completely unreliable.) Maybe this is where the vows came from. If he wanted your companionship, he'd want promises, mutual confessions, to try to make it stick. It makes sense that his breakthrough work was addressed to the first guy he'd confessed to, who didn't hate him for being queer. Allen lost his mother, but found Jack Kerouac and friends. The magnitude of the loss meant that the find couldn't simply be an inspired group of intimates; it had to give birth to something, it had to change the world. In a sense, it did. 'Howl' is also Naomi's vindication. 'The fascist national Golgotha' (Miles, 1986, p7) is real. There *are* wires in the ceiling. The secret police *are* reading your e-mail.

Allen told me he wrote 'Howl' to try to get to Kerouac. 'Howl' was, of course, much more than a note to a friend, but it's important to touch on this. Kerouac was immense for Ginsberg – an American indeed, most American of Americans for a queer commie awkward kid perpetual exile son of a mother driven mad by the pogrom and the stifling rooms of Newark. Jack was the solid exemplar of confident and serious writerly commitment, ideal poet aesthetician, football hero, able seaman, bop aficionado, and first Buddhist teacher, an instance of American manhood *not* rejected, laughed at, beaten up by the rough boys, and beautiful, Jack was beautiful. And he was kind to Allen before the drink turned him mean. So Jack's language is in the poem, particularly in the first part – angel headed ancient heavenly machinery boxcars – is pure Kerouac. When one petitions a loved one, one imitates his manners.

Ginsberg habitually presented a three-part directive to younger poets: go to the first flash of perception ('What were you thinking before you thought you were writing a poem?'), feature the details (from Blake: 'Labour well the Minute Particulars', 1988, p204), and say the secrets that everyone recognizes but dares not speak (which he associated with Reznikoff's 'each on his bed spoke to himself alone, making no sound').

In the Fifties, cutting to the first flash was in the air, its music was bop. As Zen priest and Beat affiliate Philip Whalen wrote (in his poem 'A Press Release for October, 1959'), 'This poetry is a map of the mind moving'. He could as well have been speaking of jazz or Action Painting. While Ginsberg was reading the objectivists, Kerouac was saying: 'Don't think of words when you stop, but to see the picture better' (Kerouac, 1992, p59). Allen's lifelong interest in photography makes sense in this regard. There is also a Buddhist connection – meditation as direct observation of ordinary mind rather than spacing out in some spiritual romance fit with Ginsberg's objectivist roots. Meditation was to see what one thinks; writing was to say what one sees. Allen summed up the poetical programme in 1984, when William Carlos Williams visited him in a dream and wrote:

> No need/ to dress/ it up/ as beauty/ No need/ to distort/ what's not/ standard/ to be/ understandable/ Take your/ chances/ on/ your accuracy/ Listen to/ yourself/ talk to/ yourself/ and others/ will also/ gladly/ relieved/ of the burden–/their own/ thought/ and grief./ What began/ as desire/ will end/ wiser.

('Written in my Dream by W.C.Williams',
Ginsberg, 1996, pp357-358)

The final catalyst for 'Howl' was resignation. Allen got 'Howl' from resigning his last attempt at denying his queerness (leaving his girlfriend's apartment in December '54 and moving in with Peter Orlovsky in February '55), and resigning his job in market research (May 1st '55) to devote himself to poetry. Finally (in August), the 29 year-old failed poet resigned his literary ambitions and sat down to relate a vision of their shared history to a kindred soul. Prior to writing 'Howl', Ginsberg had shown his work to Lawrence Ferlinghetti, in hope that the older poet and publisher would take him on as a City Lights author, but Lawrence declined. Then, in the autumn of 1955, Allen gave up on what he later called 'literary chatter,' and 'delivered my sermon to my soul and Jack's soul too' (to borrow a line from 'Sunflower Sutra'). And Ferlinghetti did publish 'Howl', and got busted for his efforts. And the rest, as they say…

References

Blake, William 1988 'Jerusalem', plate 55, in *The Complete Poetry and Prose of William Blake*, Newly Revised Edition, edited by David V. Erdman at <http://virtual.park.uga.edu/~wblake/eE.html> [Accessed September 5th, 2005]

Charters, Ann (ed) 1992 *The Portable Beat Reader* (New York: Viking Penguin)

Ginsberg, Allen 1996 *Selected Poems 1947-1995* (New York: Harper Collins)

Kerouac, Jack 1992 'Belief & Technique for Modern Prose' in *The Portable Beat Reader* edited by Ann Charters (New York: Viking Penguin)

Miles, Barry (ed) 1985 *Howl: Original Draft Facsimile* (New York: Harper Collins)

Schumacher, Michael 1992 *Dharma Lion: A Biography of Allen Ginsberg* (New York: St. Martin's Press)

Whalen, Philip 1999 *Overtime: Selected Poems*, edited by Michael Rothenberg (New York: Penguin Books)

Sifting the shifting sands

'Howl' and the American landscape in the 1950s

Simon Warner

On October 7th, 1955 in the Six Gallery in downtown San Francisco, an emerging but little known poet called Allen Ginsberg stood to deliver a new long poem he had been working on over the previous months. 'Howl', read to a small, if packed, crowd of friends and supporters, would-be novelists and ambitious young poets, was an immediate sensation. The listeners greeted the piece, an impassioned statement touching upon issues as broad as the Cold War, homosexuality, Buddhism and jazz, drugs, the supernatural and suicide, with a huge and enthusiastic ovation. Said Jonah Raskin in his book *American Scream: Allen Ginsberg's 'Howl' and the Making of the Beat Generation*: 'The audience was transformed [...] indifferent spectators becoming energetic participants [...] No one had been to a poetry reading that was so emotional and so cathartic' (2004, p18).

Several of the writers in attendance would actually go away and write their own first-hand account of what had gone on that evening — Jack Kerouac would fictionalise the occasion in his 1958 novel *The Dharma Bums*, for example — a suggestion in itself that there was a strong sense a piece of history, a memorable literary moment, had been played out on that autumn night. 'In all of our memories no one had been so outspoken in poetry before,' wrote another poet Michael McClure after the reading. 'We had gone beyond a point of no return — and we were ready for it, for a point of no return' (McClure, 1982, p13). An underground gathering of subterranean scribes and street philosophers, the so-called Beat Generation, had raised its head above the parapet.

With 'Howl', Ginsberg marked his arrival as a writer of profile and status. For more than ten years he had endured uncertain progress – acceptance then expulsion from the Ivy League campus of Columbia in New York, his involvement with the under-classes of Manhattan and his fringe contributions to their criminal activities, a period under the scrutiny of the asylum, his visionary episodes in which he believed he had encountered William Blake and his time as an employee of the Madison Avenue advertising industry – was behind him; his life as poet had commenced. The day after the Six Gallery reading, Lawrence Ferlinghetti, the proprietor of City Lights bookshop and its emerging publishing operation, would acknowledge Ginsberg's achievement with scant delay. Ferlinghetti, referencing words that Ralph Waldo Emerson had penned to Walt Whitman in praise of *Leaves of Grass* in 1855, exactly 100 years before, wrote to Ginsberg: 'I greet you at the beginning of a great career. When do I get the manuscript?' (Raskin, 2004, p19).

While this new era would not be without its accompanying difficulties – the acclaimed piece would indeed be published by City Lights the following year as *Howl and Other Poems* only to face obscenity charges and a high profile court case within months – the breakthrough that 'Howl' represented was enormous, not only for the writer of the poem but also those in Ginsberg's circle. His friends Kerouac and William Burroughs would gain immensely from the poet's national, then international, recognition. Ginsberg had been and remained a tireless promoter of his fellow writers' novels. He had helped Burroughs to publish his debut book, *Junkie* in 1953, and would continue to push his much more difficult, experimental works like *The Naked Lunch* as the Fifties turned into the Sixties. For Kerouac, 'Howl' was like the fanfare before the curtain rose and the stage illuminated, for Ginsberg made mention of his friend's numerous unpublished novels in the preface to the poem and included him among several dedicatees. In 1957, *On the Road*, the major novel of this tight-knit gathering of writers, would appear and cause a sensation. The Beats, a community known essentially to its core members only before the mid-1950s, would swiftly become a literary grouping familiar to hundreds and thousands of readers around the globe in the months and years that would follow.

Yet if writers and poets of a fresh vein were beginning to make their mark at this moment, there were other significant forces at play on a shifting American landscape. By the time Ginsberg premiered his soon-to-be published poem, a significant record was coming to the end of a six month stay in the Top 40, the American *Billboard* chart which had become the standard weekly sales listing for pop songs from 1940. Bill Haley and His Comets' single ('We're Gonna) Rock Around the Clock' – also widely described in its shortened version of 'Rock Around the Clock' – had entered the chart on April 15th, 1955 and would remain in that list for the next 24 weeks (Whitburn, 1983, p129). During its stay it would also enjoy 8 weeks in the Number 1 position, a significant indicator that this record had entered and remained part of the national psyche for some considerable time.

Why was this of importance? This was not Haley's first chart entry: Palmer credits his 1953 release 'Crazy Man Crazy' as 'the first white rock and roll hit' (1996, p25) and, at the end of 1954, Ward states that 'Shake, Rattle and Roll', a bowdlerised version of a Big Joe Turner hit, 'shot up the Top Ten – not only in the United States but also in England, where teenagers were apparently awaiting this blast of new music just as avidly as Americans were' (1987, pp 89-90). But 'Rock Around the Clock' left a deeper imprint because not only was it heard on record players and radios but had also been featured in an acclaimed and widely-seen movie of 1955, *The Blackboard Jungle*, a school-based drama starring Glenn Ford which had utilised music – jazz versus rock'n'roll – as a metaphor for the generation gap. The film, based on a novel by Evan Hunter concerned 'a new teacher at a high school in a "bad" section of town [who] is taunted and abused by a group of his students (including a black one played by Sidney Poitier)' (Ward, 1987, p106). A fellow teacher also endures the ignominy of having his jazz records smashed by a members of his class (*ibid*).

Why though should we attempt to elide these two works, 'Howl' and 'Rock Around the Clock', a piece of poetry and a song? Why should a connection be made between an un-minted poem, known to but a dedicated few, and a hugely successful pop record, familiar to millions across the States? This chapter will argue that both of these expressions were symptomatic of an America that was undergoing a period of dramatic transition. While Ginsberg's verse and Haley's song were coming from different intellectual places, and appealing to different sections of society, they were symbols of that metamorphosis. These two distinct tributaries in America's cultural stream gushed freely, and largely independently, during the latter 1950s and early 1960s yet, by the middle of the Sixties, appeared to find confluence. By then, the jump and jive innocence of rock'n'roll had matured into the earnest exhorting of a new rock, no longer merely concerned with the boy-meets-girl obsessions of adolescent-oriented pop but now spreading its creative net to embrace sex and psychosis, politics and pot, as the Beatles and Bob Dylan replaced the early heroes of rock's pantheon. And, with that transformation, some of the key Beats to identify that rock was something they could feed into and bounce off: the musicians and the poets would discover common ground. But that coming together is a tale for another place: here we will examine the US context in which Beat literature, with 'Howl' as its unravelling and uncompromising standard, and rock'n'roll, both symptom and cure for post-war teen neurosis, perhaps, were initially recognised.

Let us consider the national setting that applied in the middle of the 1950s and the kind of America that sustained the psychological tremors that Ginsberg's vociferous assault sent scurrying across the nation, first among the literati, then the media, then the courts and, with remarkable speed, among ordinary men and women in the street. What had been happening socially and politically prior to this thoughtquake; what had been unfolding in the worlds of literature and popular music, art and art music? The decade after the end of the Second World War, concluded first in Europe then devastatingly under atomic clouds in the Far East, was a time of extraordinary contrast for the US. On the one hand, the economic troubles that had so scarred the 1930s, troubles that had only been exorcised by a combination of Roosevelt's Keynesian plans to rebuild America and the arrival of the war which had galvanised industry and seen off the last remnants of Depression, evaporated and by the early 1950s economic boom was bringing prosperity to large portions of the nation: the white middle-classes, particularly, saw standards of living rise and the home become a haven for an abundance of newly available consumer goods – fridges and other kitchen appliances, radios and televisions. There was a sense, certainly among the advantaged sections of American society that the cruelty of war had at least been followed by the balm of material comfort, the cooling breeze of financial security. As Bradbury writes: 'Real incomes doubled, the rewards of a mass consumer society spread even further and America became a land of unprecedented affluence, an example to others. But, he counsels, 'the age of affluence was also an age of materialism and conformity' (1992, p159).

But we should be cautious of these broad brush-strokes; the picture was far from rosy in all aspects. The Civil War, that traumatic scarification of the American soul, was not yet a hundred years past and the promises the bloody conflict had intended to deliver – emancipation of the American Negro from the yolk of brutalised slavery, in particular – had only been partially fulfilled. If the barbarisms of plantation enslavement had legally ended with the war's conclusion, even by the 1950s the lot of most black men and women was only marginally improved. Mass Negro emigration to the Northern states from the 1930s and into the 1940s had seen cities like Chicago and Detroit, cradles of the US industrial recovery, employ large numbers of black workers on their production lines. In this sense there were economic prospects – jobs and homes in cities on the rise – for those who left the South even if their social position remained on the lowest reaches of the ladder. However, in the Southern states, where the wounds of the Civil War had barely healed even after the Second World War, the emancipated classes remained third-class citizens, bound in a straitjacket of so-called Jim Crow laws (see Wetterau, 1984, p419). Voting rights and educational opportunities existed in theory but, in practice, the discriminatory attitudes that persisted in Georgia, Alabama and other members of the former Confederacy meant that blacks had little chance of genuine advancement.

Not that the whites, enjoying the fruits of consumer overflow, had lives of complete security and contentment. The peace won after VE Day and VJ Day had been built on curious alliances which would quickly strain, then burst, at the seams. The enforced entente with Soviet Russia to combat Nazi Germany in Europe was rapidly revealed to be a marriage of convenience. Stalin's bootprint remained firmly planted in most of the Eastern European states that had been the battleground in the closing years of the war, the tide of Communism now spread across half the continent (Davies, 1997, pp1062-1063); the US retained a powerful military presence in the West. Germany was split four ways between the principal Allies, and Berlin, the microcosm which echoed this broader arrangement, soon emerged as the cracking point in this diplomatic stand-off. The USSR's blockade of the German capital in 1948 led to the famous air-lift to relieve those West Berliners under the administration of the Americans, French and British (*ibid*, p1067). And, of course, this was just a symptom of a wider malaise: an ideological divide between libertarian capitalism and authoritarian socialism which would become the setting for a protracted contretemps during the whole of the 1950s. Once the Rosenbergs, Julius and Ethel, had passed US nuclear secrets to the Soviets, in a bid to balance the military arsenals on each side of the split (see Wetterau, 1984, p678), the American populace spent at least a decade fearing that atomic weapons, used with such devastating event on Japan, would be targeted at them at some early stage. Nor was this fear merely a metaphorical one, simply haunting the inner psyches of America. The findings of the era's notorious McCarthy hearings appeared to go a long way to justifying these anxieties. The House Un-American Activities Committee, chaired by Senator Joseph McCarthy, suggested that Communist sympathisers were secreted in every avenue of everyday life – from politics to business, trade unions to the entertainment industry – and that these earmarked individuals were, in essence, traitors whose plotting would leave the US backdoor open and allow the Soviets to infiltrate, bringing the capitalist citadel to its knees, either through entryist stealth or invading missiles. 'Fears about communism,' says Hamilton, 'encouraged people to distrust reformers while the emergence of the prosperous suburbs, where every house looked the same, everyone watched identical television shows, and everyone dressed alike, solidified conformist views' (1997, p58).

Yet Lhamon balances the scales:

> Without denying their recent agonies, Americans were distinctly more optimistic following World War II, after taking a decade to think it all over, than during the wallows of despair that followed the trench warfare of the first war and the dislocation of the Depression. In spite of the overwhelming impact of Belsen and Nagasaki, and their warning demonstration of human capacity – mass genocide and world incineration – contemporary American culture has tried to find alternatives rather than bewail the obvious. It has tried therefore to escape the modern feeling of confinement, of complete determination, which Jean-Paul Sartre's *No Exit* so succinctly epitomised. Indeed in many of the central contemporary artefacts – *Catch-22*, Elvis Presley's 'Mystery Train', Robert Rauschenberg's combine paintings, for instance – are about this process of finding new ways to overcome despair, reassembling old feelings in new ways so to feel possibility again in the world.
>
> (1990, p7)

For black Americans, there were hints of possibility, too – the chance that they may be able to emerge from the long, dark night of political, social and economic disadvantage. For the first half of the 20th Century, the NAACP (National Association for the Advancement of Colored People), founded in 1909 (see Wetterau, 1984, p540), had been striving on behalf of the Negro population, presenting its case but making only stumbling headway. However, two developments in the middle of the decade would provide the catalyst for potential change. On the national stage, a Supreme Court ruling in the summer of 1955 would order that schools could not pursue a policy of racial segregation, a decision that would result in black schoolchildren becoming pawns in a grim game in the years that followed, as whites with a separatist inclination challenged the ruling on the streets and at the gates. But the fact was that the judiciary had backed the principle of non-discrimination, prompting a sea change in Southern American life. As Lhamon puts it: 'An agency of conservation, affirmed the radical changes already ongoing' (1990, pxii). A little later that year, when Rosa Parks refused to give up her seat to a white man 'as Southern custom demanded' (Farrell, 1997, p92) on a Montgomery, Alabama, bus, the pebble she dropped into the pool would soon build a tidal wave of activism known as the campaign for Civil Rights. That rolling programme of debate and peaceful demonstration would become a prominent focus for progressive energies, black and white, until the murder of its figurehead Martin Luther King in Memphis in 1968.

But what were the forces at play in the cultural world by the middle years of the 1950s? We have already hinted at the state of flux, but Raskin provides a lively overview to support such a proposition: 'There were visible cracks in the culture of the Cold War and sounds of liberation in rock'n'roll, in Hollywood movies like *Rebel Without a Cause*, and in plays like Arthur Miller's *A View From the Bridge* and Tennessee Williams' *Cat on a Hot Tin Roof*. There were popular novels like Sloan Wilson's *Gray Flannel Suit* that presented a critical perspective on American corporate culture, and there was provocative and innovative fiction like Vladamir Nabokov's *Lolita* first published in Paris. In baseball, the Brooklyn Dodgers defeated the New York Yankees in the 1955 World Series, an upset that showed Americans that the raggle-taggle team of bums could defeat the seemingly all-powerful machine and the men in the pinstriped uniforms' (2004, pp11-12).

Hollywood, at this time, was facing its biggest crisis since the boom days of the 1930s with the arrival of a new challenger to its hegemony. Television was an infant to cinema's adult at the start of the 1950s but it was quickly apparent that the small screen was going to be a significant threat to the much bigger one. Entertainment on TV proved to be a compelling draw to the traditional customers at whom the movie-makers had aimed their product before – adults. Consequently, the agenda of the so-called Dream Factory shifted and its studios began to make pictures which another section of the society – teenagers – would want to see. It is no coincidence that this period saw cinema walk hand-in-hand with James Dean, Marlon Brando and rock'n'roll. *Rebel Without a Cause*, *The Wild One*, and *The Blackboard Jungle* were as much about Hollywood's yearning for adolescent dollars, a means of exchange in ample supply, as a representation of the *Zeitgeist* at play, though Maltby reminds us that Hollywood also proved adept at finding other ways to manage the upstart TV. The film studios, he tells us, also 'entered television production and rapidly colonised it' (1995, p72).

In the theatre, the most important play of the time was Arthur Miller's *The Crucible* (1953), ostensibly an account of the 1692 Salem witch trials but in reality a lightly-veiled allegory for the McCarthyite investigations which had not only harried high profile people from positions of influence but demonised their friends and colleagues who had been pressurised into denouncing them. Wardle admires the playwright's technique of 'commenting on the present from the vantage point of historical melodrama' (1988, p210). The fact that Miller had been called to appear before the investigating authorities made this brave exhibition of artistic resistance particularly impressive.

In literature, in the fields of poetry and the novel, what had been the trends in the years before Ginsberg's 'Howl' exploded? Bradbury talks of the situation at the end of the Second World War as the beginning of 'the age of American hegemony' (1992, p159). Modernism had died, he argues, with the passing of Yeats and Freud in 1939, Joyce and Woolf in 1941. In the US, the fall-out from the war's paradoxical political alliances had a bearing on the way the written word evolved. He remarks: 'It is significant that the very best of the post-war American writers were those who had acquired their political education in the left-wing atmosphere of the 1930s and were now in the process of coming to terms with the atmosphere of moral ambiguity that ran so strongly through the post-war, cold war atmosphere of the late 1940s and 1950s, when writers throughout the West felt writing needed to begin again' (*ibid*, p164). The searing jolt of the Holocaust prompted a string of Jewish intellectuals, who had tarried with Communism and then left it behind, to express their feelings through fiction. He cites Saul Bellow, Norman Mailer, Bernard Malamud and Philip Roth as important examples of this trend. 'Now the theme was no longer the immigrant victim struggling for place and recognition in the New World, rather that of the Jew as modern victim forced by history into existential self-definition, a definition that was not solely religious, political, or ethnic' (*ibid*, p165). Cunliffe suggests that Bellow, Malamud, Mailer and Ginsberg 'all of them in their individual ways [...] developed techniques of writing-as-talk (confession, harangue, invective)' that departed 'radically from the well-behaved, consistent locutions of the genteel tradition' (1986, p401). Mailer would, a little further down the road, publish his widely read essay 'The White Negro' in 1957, which contemplated the white need to emulate black behaviour and values. Meanwhile, black fiction, represented best by Ralph Ellison's *Invisible Man* (1952) and James Baldwin's *Go Tell it On the Mountain* (1953) and *Giovanni's Room* (1956) also revealed the rise of a Negro voice that explored a morality that was charged with a sense of political outrage, as identity, religion and sexuality were addressed from the other side of the racial tracks.

Yet there is little doubt that the book which would cast most light on the crisis facing neurotic affluent white America would come from the pen of J.D.Salinger in the form of 1951's *The Catcher in the Rye*. Bradbury says that 'the moral and realistic novel of the 1950s was always a novel under strain, under pressure from ethical change, sexual expectation, and changing attitudes to personal fulfilment, and above all from the ever-complicating American reality' and it was Salinger's book that perhaps best expressed this quality of tension. He calls it 'the strongest novel of the Fifties; it caught its mood and became a universal student classic' (1992, p180). Cunliffe says that the novel 'seemed to speak for an era which distrusted public attitudes but had nothing very certain to put in their place (1988, p392). Salinger 'seemed *the* voice of the youthful, middle-class urban American' whose central character Holden Caulfield 'surveys Manhattan and its hinterland through the eyes of an incoherent but likeably honest teenager' (Cunliffe, 1986, pp413-414).

As for poetry, those pillars of modernism, Ezra Pound and T.S. Eliot, still cast long shadows over the years that followed the

Second World War yet their status and reception was confused, perhaps compromised, by their allegiances, political and national. Pound's dalliance with fascism tarnished his poetic reputation; Eliot's decision to take British citizenship in 1927 would alter perceptions among those of his original homeland. It is intriguing that William Carlos Williams should criticise the pair suggesting that by 'kowtowing to Europe' they had both harmed American poetry (Cunliffe, 1986, p419). Williams from the same New Jersey town, Paterson, as Ginsberg, would not only leave his own mark on American verse but would become friend, mentor and influence on the younger poet.

While we might mention noted poetic figures of this period – Robert Lowell, John Berryman and Marianne Moore and the emerging nexus at Black Mountain College – the importance of Williams, a practising doctor who remained a working poet throughout his life, to Ginsberg, cannot be underestimated. Williams was also more than a versifier; his theorising on poetry affected a number of young poets including the individual who would eventually unveil 'Howl'. Explains Mottram: 'Williams' example was effective right through the 1950s and into the 1960s – a long example by poetry and writing on poetry [...] Poetry for him [...] was not simply personal lyricism and imitations of regular measures and stanzas: it was an innovating function of society. The line of speech is the basic measure, a form which excludes no possibility of intelligent resource. The form is not 'free verse' but the measure and spatial control of cadential lengths and the varied placing of a wide range of information' (1988, pp242-243). He refers to Williams' own cycle, *Paterson*, in five books between 1946 and 1958, to typify this manner of expression and adds: 'In 1948 Williams wrote of a poem as 'a field of action'; these works carry the sense of a constructed place to work, into which the poet's experience is continuously articulated, becoming synonymous with his life, rather than in the sense of the alchemist engaged for life in his work' (*ibid*, p243). William Carlos Williams became a friend and guide to the young Ginsberg and, when 'Howl' was published as the centrepiece of Ginsberg's debut collection, the older man would pen the foreword.

In the visual arts, the 1950s would see seismic shifts in aesthetic attitudes. At the start, the predominance of Abstract Expressionism, the ultimate statement of the abstract concerns of the modernist ethos as represented by Jackson Pollock, Barnett Newman and Mark Rothko, was evident. The decline of the representational, the realistic or figurative, had been in progress for the first half of the century but when Pollock, specifically, pursued a new style from 1947 involving the pouring or dripping of paint on to the canvas, 'he dissolved the customary compositional focus on a central image and broke down the illusion of objects in space, arriving at an 'allover' composition in which the seemingly limitless intricacy of surface texture creates a vast, pulsating environment of intense energy, completely engulfing the viewer' (Fineberg, 2000, p86). Yet if this loosely-tied American school retained a kudos in the opening years of the decade, by the mid-point, a counter-revolution would gain crucial momentum. Pop Art would challenge the notions of existential abstraction, adopting rather than rejecting the objects of mass society. Robert Rauschenberg, whose early work at Black Mountain College, owed much more to abstraction than the semiotics of Pop, would eventually, alongside Jasper Johns, help trigger a movement that would draw freely on the imagery of the movies and billboards, comic books and supermarket shelves. Their heirs, Andy Warhol, Roy Lichtenstein, James Rosenquist and others, would produce artworks which represented 'the first cultural flowering of postmodernism' (Sim, 1998, pp147-148), as the processes of high art became fervently engaged with the semiotics of mass production and consumption, paying homage and lampooning them in an intriguing sleight of hand.

Musically, the early 1950s would see John Cage, another Black Mountain activist, as the exemplar of the modernist impulse. His *Music of Changes* had been a ground-breaking experiment in 1951. The following year, his production *Theater Piece #1*, which also incorporated Rauschenberg's minimal 'White Paintings' and Merce Cunningham's choreography, became regarded as the first 'happening' (Fineberg, 2000, p176). Yet in less rarefied circles – in the cities, on the streets, in the bars and concert venues – the sounds of America were undergoing a thrilling evolution. Dramatic developments such as bebop, the chosen style of most of the Beat circle, would maintain its momentum as the cutting edge of jazz. In the 1940s Kerouac and his Manhattan friends were first-hand witnesses to this process, as Charlie Parker and Dizzy Gillespie, Charles Mingus and Thelonius Monk brought a new frenetic sound to the clubs of Manhattan's 52nd Street and the uptown venues of Harlem. Their tempestuous improvisation left the formal features of swing and the big band far behind, a sign that the Negro artist could still speak with a voice that was fiercely individual, determinedly original, in the face of widespread artistic appropriation by white band-leaders and musicians. For Ralph Ellison, bebop marked nothing less than 'a momentous modulation into a new key of musical sensibility; in brief, a revolution in culture' (cited in DeVeaux, 1999, p1). When Kerouac and Ginsberg sought means to reflect the fracture and fury of the world around them in their writing, the pulse and patter of jazz phrasing served their prose and poetry well.

Yet, to return to earlier themes in this essay, if bebop, and the bigger umbrella of modern jazz, was the soundtrack to a particular

41

cool urban clique, a crowd aware of Miles Davis, of marijuana and maybe the attitudes framed in the French existential literature of the time – Sartre and Albert Camus – then younger, mainstream audiences across the US were discovering a musical hybrid that veered toward the visceral rather than the cerebral. Rock'n'roll, long-time black slang for the sexual act, represented a cross-fertilisation of genres that had not found common ground until the early 1950s. Blues and R&B, the sounds of Negro America, had been broadly confined to black audiences, segregated in their own 'race' chart. Country music, a style which had been dubbed hillbilly in its early incarnations then called Country&Western as the form expanded from its roots in the South to the new states in the West, was associated with white consumers. Yet this period was ripe for change and the barriers would not remain in place for long. When musicians and managers, producers and promoters, black and white, blues and country, intermingled in centres like Memphis, where the North met the South, the chemistry would forge alliances and provide new opportunities. As Palmer states: 'A new breed of American musicians and entrepreneurs found the literal and imaginative space to create something fresh' (1996, pp16-17).

The stimuli for this changing climate had been triggered in the 1940s. A number of industrial and technological factors had paved the way for a transformed popular music scene. At the start of that decade the four national radio stations became embroiled in a dispute with the biggest royalty collecting operation ASCAP – the American Society of Composers, Authors and Publishers. When the artists body sought higher rates for airplay, the radio companies refused and a strike ensued. The vast majority of the most significant song repertoire became unavailable to the airwaves. But the radio stations did not capitulate. Instead they set up a new royalty operation called the BMI, Broadcast Music Incorporated (see Palmer, 1996, p136). This new agency did not restrict itself to songwriters in the dominating Broadway tradition of Gershwin, Porter and Kern. Blues, R&B, country and Latin composers had the chance to be played and earn from their music in a way that would have been quite unlikely without the ASCAP dispute. When the industrial disagreements were settled – and the process took around two years – the old monopolies were broken and BMI artists had their foot in the door.

Other factors would play their part in the creation of records – the re-emergence of independent labels, the rise of television and its surprising side effects and the invention of vinyl, a versatile and longer-lasting material that emerged from war-time plastics research. Independent labels were first called so in the 1940s. The Wall Street Crash of 1929 had seen dozens of small record labels collapse. Only the biggest players, companies like RCA, Decca and EMI – eventually dubbed the majors – would survive. As the Depression ebbed and war erupted, a new generation of immigrant businessmen moved into the sector creating small operations which took particular interest in musical styles at the fringes – the blues, jazz and R&B. Thus the Bihari brothers from Lebanon established Modern in Los Angeles, the Turkish Ertegun brothers founded Atlantic in New York and, in Chicago, the Chess brothers from Poland built their eponymous record company (see Gillett, 1987, pp67-118). Through these outlets performers like Muddy Waters, Big Joe Turner, Ruth Brown, Little Walter and John Lee Hooker would gain national profiles.

Television would play a curious and accidental role in opening up the musical channels. When TV's foothold grew at the end of the 1940s there was a widespread assumption that radio would go into quick decline – who would want to merely listen when images and sound were available in tandem? 'Many experts,' says Peterson, 'reasoning that no one would listen to a box when they could listen to a box that also showed moving pictures, thought that TV would completely replace radio' (1990, p102). One result of this was that radio licences, previously highly prized, expensive and hard to obtain, were now off-loaded much more cheaply and easily in a bid to squeeze out a last gasp return before their value collapsed (see Peterson, 1990). The consequence was that many licences were issued to smaller, niche operators whose interest lay in playing fringe musical styles. This gave further impetus to the rise of genres that had previously been marginalised. Radio transmitters became more powerful, too. When Cleveland radio DJ Alan Freed – the man who claimed to have coined the term rock'n'roll in a musical context – presented his *Moondog House* show replete with R&B sounds, favourable weather conditions could carry the Ohio broadcast to New York listeners. Crucially, white teenagers could hear black records on air for the first time, constructing a new market for sounds that had been previously enjoyed only in Negro parts of town. This novel interplay, this cross-cultural alchemy, would open avenues in the early to mid-Fifties quite unthinkable in 1945.

So, in our bid to consider the environment in which Ginsberg's 'Howl', and 'Rock Around the Clock', too, made their initial impressions, we have contemplated, by way of summary, the social and the economic, the political and racial, the artistic, literary and theatrical, entertainment interests as represented by Hollywood, by radio and television, the poetical and the musical. We may have gone further, of course, and weighed up the role of matters as diverse as sex and sexuality, drugs and spirituality, for instance, in the shaping of a fresh consciousness, but the areas examined, I would argue, provide a useful framework of understanding. In what ways, then, can we draw lines between the poetic and musical texts under scrutiny and the broader setting outlined within this account? How did issues of black and white, middle-class affluence and consumer boom, Cold War stresses and political witch-hunts, the rise of television and a new wave of movie star rebels, teenage identity and adolescent spending power, have a bearing on what Ginsberg recited or Haley sang? In short, the poem and the song teased out many of the tensions, many of the concerns, many of the excitements that the new America was experiencing. Old certainties – racial groupings, political alliances, respect of the flag and authority and deference to age – were no longer so well-founded and these cultural landmarks suggested as much.

Bill Haley's release reflected the move from the white ballad to a more rhythmic style propelled by an insistent back-beat. Those characteristics owed much to the R&B and jump jive traditions of the black community of the 1940s and early 1950s, but there had been a softening, a smoothing out of the Negro qualities: the earthier elements had been toned down. This was something that Haley had already engaged in on earlier recorded outings. When he took Big Joe Turner's 'Shake Rattle and Roll' in 1954, a track which shared similar musical and production ingredients to 'Rock Around the Clock', he had followed a familiar route by sanitising lyrics that were felt too sexually explicit in their original form. But the fact that these stylistic features or hints of innuendo could feature in a white artist's repertoire, and then be propelled into the charts, were clear indicators of change. The message of 'Rock Around the Clock' was certainly subversive. Stepping away from the debate around the word rock – did it mean dance or was there a sexual sub-text to that term? – the song expressed that adolescent ambition to escape the restrictions of the clock and curfew, home life and respectability. When *The Blackboard Jungle* utilised Haley's song and live performance to personify the new concerns of American youth – a desire to knock over the old, an aspiration to independence, a keenness to create a distinct identity from the adult world – a platform for the song's widespread exposure was well and truly built. Little Richard or Chuck Berry, already enjoying some success by this time, may have better represented this new youthful fervour but their blackness would have been too threatening for the Hollywood companies making the picture and the vast majority of the audience which came to view it. Haley, kiss-curled but far from youthful leading a group which through its horns also featured unprovocative hints of a white swing act, became the conduit by which more potent representatives of the black/white crossover – like Berry, Elvis Presley and Jerry Lee Lewis – could later raise their performing and recording profiles. 'Rock Around the Clock' was a pervasive, accessible courier of a new spirit, heard by tens of millions, but it was more emblem than manifesto.

Allen Ginsberg's epic work was more complex, more densely wrought, more fraught, more personal in tone and content. It eschewed the metaphorical, refused to side-step the unsayable, and confronted in a direct, not to say courageous, fashion the crisis facing the outsider in America. Ginsberg, as son of Socialist father and Communist mother and someone who had held earlier ambitions to become a labour lawyer, had sufficient Leftist credentials to place himself in McCarthy's firing line. If the poet had emerged five years earlier he would have very likely faced the wrath of the HUAC and maybe suffered the kind of fate that the great campaigning folk singer Pete Seeger endured during the 1950s – banned from the airwaves, banned from performing, facing the constant threat of imprisonment. But Ginsberg, in 1955, was more than just a political agitant, a potential speck of grit in the establishment's eye. As a Jew and as a homosexual man – and 'Howl' is, among so many things, a baring of the poet's sexual soul

– Ginsberg was doubly, triply, cursed in the mainstream view of this WASP-dominated society. Yet, typically, Ginsberg does not pen a verse merely bemoaning his own dilemma – he includes himself in this drama, inspired by those very principles William Carlos Williams had discussed with him as he sought to break away from formal poetics and develop his own voice – but presents a universal appeal on behalf of the marginalised, disenfranchised, the dispossessed, the lost American, black or white, clinging by broken fingernails to the last carriages of the affluence express. Yet 'Howl' is also a celebration of that listless, anxious, wandering America which seeks new truths, fresh hope, through music, drugs, spirituality and travel, away from the threat of arrest, of surveillance, of banishment. The work is an eclectic gathering of the ancient and the modern, which gives a poem that was the height of contemporary commentary in 1955, a timeless durability. As Mottram states: 'His measure is frequently a large inclusive line, reaching sometimes paragraphic proportions, a major inventive rhetoric of the time, and eminently suited to declamation. It incorporated Melville's sentence structure […], Hebraic scripture, Blake's long lines and Whitman's chants' (1988, p270).

How might we then sum up this meeting of two diverse artefacts of expression and the extraordinary period into which they were thrown? How can we measure their impact? There is no doubt both 'Howl' and 'Rock Around the Clock' left a heavy thumbprint on that decade. The poem – its reading and publication, its obscenity trial and the subsequent acquittal – gave the Beat writers an opportunity to present and explain their philosophies nationally and globally. The impact of those ideas on cultural and sub-cultural life in the next 15 years were huge, informing the growing folk revival and Civil Rights movement, the rock revolution of the mid-1960s, the rise of the hippies and the anti-Vietnam War struggles. Ginsberg's ideologies and his active presence formed a cornerstone to the counterculture in the US and in Europe. As for the song, it enjoyed transatlantic success and, as we have proposed, opened doors for more captivating, more charismatic, performers than Haley. It is hard to see how rock'n'roll would have won such a following, so quickly, without that artist and without that release. By extension, it is also difficult to see how figures of the stature of Bob Dylan and the Beatles could have emerged without the conjunctions of Beat verse and rock'n'roll music, without the 1955 successes of 'Howl' and 'Rock Around the Clock'. By the end of the Fifties, Dylan was as interested in Kerouac and Ginsberg as he was in Little Richard and Woody Guthrie; John Lennon was an art-school follower of both Beat writing and Gene Vincent. By the mid-1960s, Ginsberg was warmly welcomed into their near regal circles.

But, to step into the present half a century later, does the distant pulse of those happenings still register on our cultural geiger-counter? In these postmodern times, can we retrospectively see that poem and that song, as important contributors to our contemporary condition, our latterday frame of mind? For Jameson postmodernism's existence rests on 'the hypothesis of some radical break [...] generally traced back to the end of the 1950s or he early 1960s. As the word [postmodernism] itself suggests, this break is most often related to notions of the waning or extinction of the hundred-year-old modern movement [...] Thus Abstract Expressionism in painting, existentialism in philosophy, the final forms of representation in the novel, the films of the great *auteurs*, or the modernist school of poetry [...] all are now seen as the final extraordinary flowering of a high-modernist impulse which is spent and exhausted with them' (1999, pp1-2). In the early 21st Century, in an age when older understandings of cultural – and social – order have been rent asunder, certainly reshuffled almost beyond recognition, was the mid-1950s a time when those realignments were well and truly set in train?

Rock'n'roll, the marrying of white and black styles – country and blues – has been occasionally posited as a moment when popular music and the postmodern initially converged, ideas outlined by Strinati (1995, pp233-235). Here were two separate threads – each borrowing from the other – and producing a collage of styles. Strinati suggests that rock'n'roll was 'a novel and original fusion' and therefore not postmodern but if we are to widen the scope of our analysis and put the stress, instead, on Jameson's 'radical break', then the production and consumption of this new music, both of which side-stepped the long-standing racial boundaries, did represent a very significant break with older working traditions. The Beats, in a different way, could be regarded as precursors of the postmodern, too. Their radical approaches to literary content and form, their methods of presentation and dissemination, have contributed to the crumbling of the walls between high and low art. How did they do this? They celebrated the anecdotal and autobiographical; they favoured the candid and confessional; they rejected the formalism of the academy; they took their poetry to bars and cafes; and they self-published and spread their work through little magazines outside the publishing establishment. In short, they kicked over the traces of convention at every turn.

Ginsberg's poetry, never unhappy to reflect on and include the symbols and signs of the everyday, has, in that sense, a relationship to the Pop artists, another creative community whose work has helped to shape the debate on the shift to postmodernity, as we have already mentioned. The mid and latter years of the 1950s were a time when American society was still repressed and rigid – the presence in the White House of Dwight Eisenhower, a military man with powerful links to the triumphs and traumas of the Second World War embodied this – but the artistic shifts, a series of potent undercurrents, were strongly suggesting the decade to follow would be somewhat different. 'Howl' and 'Rock Around the Clock' were, undoubtedly, significant, early signs. So was Arthur Miller's marriage to Marilyn Monroe – the avatar of legitimate theatre marrying a screen goddess and, perhaps *the* popular icon of the era – and so were Miles Davis' new takes on Joaquín Rodrigo and Manuel de Falla when the *Sketches of Spain* sessions began at the very end of the decade. The *ancien régime* of high-brow and low-brow, elite and popular, was gradually crumbling, a preface to a moment, not far off, when Ginsberg and Dylan could establish shared agendas and Andy Warhol would feel able to invite the Velvet Underground into his own palace of mysteries.

References

Bradbury, Malcolm 1992 *The Modern American Novel*, 2nd Edition (Oxford: Opus)

Cunliffe, Marcus 1986 *The Literature of the United States*, 4th Edition (Harmondsworth: Penguin)

Cunliffe, Marcus (ed) 1988 *American Literature Since 1900* (London: Sphere)

Davies, Norman 1997 *Europe: A History* (London: Pimlico)

DeVeaux, Scott 1997 *The Birth of Bebop: A Social and Musical History* (London: Picador)

Farrell, James J. 1997 *The Spirit of the Sixties: The Making of Postwar Radicalism* (London: Routledge)

Feldman, Gene and Max Gartenberg 1960 *Protest: The Beat Generation and the Angry Young Men* (London: Panther)

Fineberg, Jonathan 2000 *Art Since 1940: Strategies of Being* (London: Laurence King)

Gillett, Charlie 1987 *The Sound of the City* (London: Souvenir)

Ginsberg, Allen 1960 'Howl' in *Protest: The Beat Generation and the Angry Young Men*, edited by Gene Feldman and Max Gartenberg (London: Panther)

Hamilton, Neil A. 1997 *The ABC-CLIO Companion to the 1960s Counterculture in America* (Santa Barbara, CA: ABC-CLIO)

Jameson, Fredric 1999 *Postmodernism or the Cultural Logic of Late Capitalism* (Durham, North Carolina: Duke University Press)

Lhamon, Jr, W.T. 1990 *Deliberate Speed: The Origins of a Cultural Style in the American 1950s* (London: Smithsonian Institution)

McClure, Michael 1982 *Scratching the Beat Surface* (San Francisco: North Point Press)

Maltby, Richard 1995 *Hollywood Cinema* (Oxford: Blackwell)

Mottram, Eric 1988 'American Poetry, Poetics and Poetic

Movements' in *American Literature Since 1900*, edited by Marcus Cunliffe (London: Sphere)

Palmer, Robert 1996 *Dancing in the Street: A Rock & Roll History* (London: BBC Books)

Peterson, Richard A. 1990 'Why 1955? Explaining the advent of rock music' in *Popular Music* 9/1

Raskin, Jonah 2004 *American Scream: Allen Ginsberg's 'Howl' and the Making of the Beat Generation* (London: University of California Press)

Sim, Stuart 1998 *The Icon Dictionary of Postmodern Thought* (Cambridge: Icon)

Strinati, Dominic 1995 *An Introduction to Theories of Popular Culture* (London: Routledge)

Ward, Ed 1987 'The Fifties and Before' in *Rock of Ages: The Rolling Stone History of Rock and Roll*, edited by Ed Ward, Geoffrey Stokes and Ken Tucker (London: Penguin)

Ward, Ed, Geoffrey Stokes and Ken Tucker 1987 *Rock of Ages: The Rolling Stone History of Rock and Roll* (London: Penguin)

Wardle, Irving 1988 'American Theatre since 1945' in *American Literature Since 1900*, edited by Marcus Cunliffe (London: Sphere)

Wetterau, Bruce (ed) 1984 *Concise Dictionary of World History* (London: Robert Hale) Whitburn, Joel 1983 *The Billboard Book of US Top 40 Hits – 1955 to Present* (New York: Billboard Publications)

The dramatic imagery of 'Howl'
The [naked] bodies of madness

George Rodosthenous

...the suffering of America's naked mind for love
into an eli eli lamma lamma sabacthani
saxophone cry that shivered the cities

('Howl', 1956)

Unlike Arthur Rimbaud who wrote his 'A Season in Hell' (1873) when he was only 19 years-old, Allen Ginsberg was 29 when he completed his epic poem 'Howl' (1956). Both works encapsulate an intense world created by the imagery of words and have inspired and outraged their readers alike. What makes 'Howl' relevant to today, 50 years after its first reading, is its honest and personal perspective on life, and its nearly journalistic, but still poetic, approach to depicting a world of madness, deprivation, insanity and jazz. And in that respect, it would be sensible to point out the similarities of Rimbaud's concerns with those of Ginsberg's. They both managed to create art that changed the *status quo* of their times and confessed their nightmares in a way that inspired future generations. Yet there is a stark contrast here: for Rimbaud, 'A Season in Hell' was his swan song; fortunately, in the case of Ginsberg, he continued to write for decades longer, until his demise in 1997.

Even if more than three quarters of a century had elapsed following Rimbaud's publication of his 'catabasis' to hell, even if the world had been changed by two global conflicts, the rebellious concerns of Ginsberg seem similar to the ones that had engaged that youthful visionary of the previous century. In each instance, there was an urgent need to run away from the system, flee the routine, engineer a strategy of escapism through art. This escapist impulse represented a life that could be lived to its full intensity, with no rules and regulations, with excesses and boundary-less excursion. Ginsberg's world is full of dramatic imagery, 'sound and fury' which attack the reader and enclose him in a claustrophobic environment of people who are in desperate need of a change – a personal revolution. In order to discuss the ways I approached the reading of 'Howl', I borrowed some of Michael McClure's impressions of the poem as sub-headings for my article. Also, for the purposes of this publication, I will limit my discussion only to the first part of 'Howl'.

New intensity

> Allen began in a small and intensely lucid voice. At some point Jack Kerouac began shouting 'GO' in cadence as Allen read it. In all our memories no one had been so outspoken by poetry before – we had gone beyond a point of no return – and we were ready for it, for a point of no return.
>
> (McClure, 1982, p13)

The intensity of the visual imagery of 'Howl' is undeniable. Even 50 years later, the reader is bombarded with explosions of images, some of an explicit nature. It would be fascinating to try and imagine the reaction on the faces of those 150 or so gathered in October 1955 to listen to this work for the first time. The sounds of the words are translated into images with such strength and the images become a synaesthetic experience which opens up the worlds of juxtaposed dreams and nightmares. The musical references play an integral part in this verbal stream of consciousness. The rhythms of the sounds, the hypnotic and, at times, seductive colour of the images, provide the canvas on which a chapter in American history is drawn in a most provocative, shameless and unapologetic way. The barrage of images could, at first, be suffocating, but the after-taste of 'Howl''s opening section is the soothing image of a lonely solo saxophone. The saxophone is the representative of solitude – 'What solitude I've finally inherited' (Ginsberg, 'Siesta in Xbalba', 1954) – and its loneliness doubles up as the representative of an individual spiritual revolution. With its cry, the saxophone states its own manifesto against society and the norm. This image echoes the passage from Kerouac's *On the Road* where,

> The tenorman jumped down from the platform and stood in the crowd, blowing around; his hat was over his eyes; somebody pushed it back for him. He just hauled back and stamped his foot and blew down a hoarse baughing blast, and drew breath, and raised the horn and blew high, wide, and screaming in the air. Dean was directly in front of him with his face lowered to the bell of the horn, clapping his hands, pouring sweat on the man's keys, and the man noticed and laughed in his horn a long quivering crazy laugh, and everybody else laughed and they rocked and rocked; and finally the tenorman decided to blow his top and crouched down and held a note in high C for a long time as everything else crashed along and the cries increased and I thought the cops would come swarming from the nearest precinct. Dean was in a

trance. The tenorman's eyes were fixed straight on him; he had a madman who not only understood but cared and wanted to understand more and much more than there was, and they began dueling for this...

(1957, p197)

The detailed description of the music night-scene must have given a visual impulse to many artists (and probably to Anthony Minghella for his famous jazz-club scene in the 1999 film *The Talented Mr Ripley*) where through the intensity of experiencing live music, the act of listening itself cements the male bonding of the characters. This homosocial activity counter-balances the lack of the homosocial activity of sport.

The saxophone cry breaks the boundaries and elates the atmosphere to one of anarchic intensity, power and muscular masculinity. It is identified with freedom from 'serious' classical musical and elevates improvisation into a valid art form which, even though is difficult to document and preserve (because it can only exist in the moment), is tremendous to experience. And, in part, that was the novelty of the Beat Generation.

Escapism – visionary [musical] voices of freedom

None of us wanted to go back to the gray, chill, militaristic silence, to the intellective void – to the land without poetry – to the spiritual drabness. We wanted to make it new and we wanted to invent it and the process of it as we went into it. We wanted voice and we wanted vision.

(McClure, 1982, p13)

Ginsberg was opposed to the militaristic silence of the non-rebel and other kinds of discipline enforced by the system. He, like his other fellow contemporary poets, preferred the expressive freedom of jazz music. The rhythm of the military drum becomes the swinging brush of the jazz band. The structural monotony of military silence is transformed, instead, into the extreme freedom of improvisation, where everything is acceptable, the rules are there to be broken and to be re-invented on the way. A mistake can be changed to an intentional feature of the work, repeated, developed, discarded or abandoned. In that respect, his work is full of rhythms, cadences and solo extemporisations on specific themes: the liberation of the lustful body is what he described most explicitly and celebrated throughout his life.

Rimbaud, in his 'A Season in Hell' acknowledged the need of the younger generations to break free from the constraints of society, to travel and experience new truths. Whether Ginsberg is regarded as prophet or punk, the tie that connects the two poets is their determination to change the poetry of their age by reflecting on personal experiences and honing them to become diachronic pieces of diary art. These voices became the leading voices of freedom of their generation and created their own school of thought which tried to change the *status quo* through poetry and the power of the words.

Ginsberg also acknowledges the power of music in his determination to up-turn the world. In 'Howl', he writes about people 'who sat in boxes breathing in the darkness under the bridge, and rose up to build harpsichords in their lofts', and 'who sang out of their windows in despair'. The power of music to bring social change and improvement, the power of being able to look at the past, represented in the poem by the harpsichord, re-build it and then with that knowledge and experience of tradition create new works of art is essential for any culture. The musical imagery creates its own dialectic and invites the reader to think of sounds to accompany his reading of the poem. So, a reading of 'Howl' is not only embellished with saxophone sounds, but with the sounds of harpsichords being built, tuned and played and sad (ethnic) songs are sung to create the new voices which will cry out for freedom. The music works on a sub-conscious level within the rhythm of the poem and adds colour and dissonance with 'pushcarts full of onions and bad music': a contemporary hymn to freedom.

Unveiling the unspoken

At a reading…in Los Angeles…one particular heckler harassed Ginsberg throughout his reading [of 'Howl'] and was quieted only when Allen promised to give him the chance to express his opinions after the reading. However he continued to disrupt the reading after Allen had turned it over to [Gregory] Corso. At one point, Gregory proposed a verbal duel with the heckler, the winner being the one with the best 'images, metaphors (and) magic'. The heckler was more interested in engaging Corso in a fistfight. He taunted the poets, calling them cowards, insisting they explain what they were trying to prove onstage.

'Nakedness,' Ginsberg replied. When the heckler demanded further explanation, Allen left the stage and approached him. He accused the man of wanting to do something brave in front of the audience and then challenged him to take off all his clothes. As he walked towards the drunk, Allen stripped off all of his

clothing, hurling his pants and shirt at the now retreating
heckler. 'Stand naked before the people,' Allen said. 'The
poet always stands naked before the world'. Defeated
the man backed into another room.

(Schumacher, 1992, p242)

It is no surprise that the *Times Literary Supplement* has written that
'[n]o one has made his poetry speak for the whole man, without
inhibition of any kind, more than Ginsberg'. He had this gift of
exploring the deepest fantasies and sharing them with his reader in
a hypnotic way, which no other versifier has done since the Greek
poet Constantine Cavafy (1863-1933) at the beginning of the 20th
Century. Cavafy was more discrete in his writing, but one of his
main recurring themes was the body remembering erotic
experiences of the past:

> Body, remember not only how much you were loved
> not only the beds you lay on,
> but also those desires glowing openly
> in eyes that looked at you,
> trembling for you in voices –
> only some chance obstacle frustrated them.
> Now that it's all finally in the past,
> it seems almost as if you gave yourself
> to those desires too – how they glowed,
> remember, in eyes that looked at you,
> remember, body, how they trembled for you in those voices.

('Body remember', 1919)

It could be argued that Ginsberg even borrows some of Cavafy's
meta-poetical narrative where the erotic experience is documented

as soon as it takes place. The Greek poet's imagery leaves no ambiguity regarding the intentions and content of the activities described:

> Their illicit pleasure has been fulfilled.
> They get up and dress quickly, without a word.
> They come out of the house separately, furtively;
> and as they move off down the street a bit unsettled,
> it seems they sense that something about them betrays
> what kind of bed they've just been lying on.
> But what profit for the life of the artist:
> tomorrow, the day after, or years later, he'll give voice
> to the strong lines that had their beginning here.
>
> ('Their beginning', 1921)

Ginsberg's 'Love Poem on a Theme by Whitman' (1954), 'Many Loves' (1956) and 'Please Master' (1968) are only a few samples from the treasures of erotic, forbidden poetry that he has left behind. These works' explicit language and imagery are integrated in a more toned down language in 'Howl'. 'Publishing obscene odes' could be a way to characterise some of Ginsberg's own work since he lays bare the body in an unashamedly explicit way in a large proportion of his work. His fascination with the naked body invites the reader to an orgasmic world of words and images. In 'Love Poem on a Theme by Whitman', inspired by a drawing of Robert LaVigne and reflecting on his imagined, ideal involvement with one of Neal Cassady's weddings, he writes:

> I'll go into the bedroom silently and lie down between
> the bridegroom and the bride,
> those bodies fallen from heaven stretched out watching

naked and restless,
arms resting over their eyes in the darkness,
bury my face in their shoulders and breasts,
breathing their skin[…]
and the bride cry for forgiveness, and the groom be
covered with tears of passion and compassion,
and I rise form the bed replenished with last intimate
gestures and kisses of farewell –
all before the mind wakes, behind shades and closed
doors in a darkened house
where the inhabitants roam unsatisfied in the night,
nude ghosts seeking each other out in the silence.

('Love Poem on a Theme by Whitman', 1954)

Homoerotic imagery is also featured in 'Howl' with images of men 'who cowered in unshaven rooms in underwear', 'who broke down crying in white gymnasiums naked and trembling before the machinery of other skeletons' who 'sob behind a partition in a Turkish bath when the blond & naked angel came to pierce them with a sword'. Nakedness and nudity, exposing the private, 'waving genitals and manuscripts', 'scattering semen freely', men 'who copulated ecstatic and insatiate with a bottle of beer' provide unveiled images of the human body which proved to be extremely controversial at the time. Paul Breslin writes about Ginsberg's approach to poetic nakedness in his book *The Psycho-Political Muse* that:

> 'Madness' seems choosy about its victims, singling out
> the best minds to destroy; perhaps they go mad *because*
> they are the best minds. The three adjectives perched on
> the end of the line – 'starving hysterical naked' – may at
> first seem mere overwriting. But they suggest that these

elect 'best minds' are 'starving' not only for food, drugs, and sex, but for spiritual transcendence, for 'the ancient heavenly connection to the starry dynamo in the machinery of night'. Such yearning seems mystical only to a society that represses its own hunger for spiritual (as well as sexual) exploration. They are 'naked' not only in their refusal to wear the clothes of social convention, or in preparation for lovemaking, but also in their vulnerability. In refusing all covering, they refuse protection also. The best minds have no Reichian character armor. And although 'minds' stands metonymically for persons and emphasizes consciousness rather than the body, these 'minds' are presented in predominantly bodily terms: one thinks of the body in connection with the words 'naked' and 'starving', and even 'hysterical' derives from the Greek word for 'womb'. The hysterias that Freud decided to treat psychologically had previously been considered somatic ailments. The effect of Ginsberg's language is to sexualize the concept of 'mind', making it more bodily and instinctive, while simultaneously spiritualizing the body, making its hunger and nakedness into emblems of religious yearning.

(Breslin, 1987, p7)

Neal Cassady, Ginsberg's eternal muse, features in 'Howl' as well as in other poems which are entirely dedicated to him, for example 'Elegy for Neal Cassady' (1968) and the moving 'On Neal's Ashes' (1968). 'N.C., secret hero of these poems, cocksman and Adonis of Denver' refers to the activities of a man who was such a:

joy to the memory of his innumerable lays of girls in
empty lots & diner backyards, moviehouses' rickety
rows, on mountaintops in caves or with gaunt waitresses
in familiar roadside lonely petticoat upliftings &
especially secret gas-station solipsisms of johns, &
hometown alleys too

('Howl', 1956)

These images remind us of the description featured in another
poem of the same period mentioned above and called 'Many
Loves' (1956). In 'Many Loves' there are vivid descriptions of
Cassady's body where 'his belly of fists and starvation, his belly a
thousand girls kissed in Colorado, his belly of rocks thrown over
Denver roofs, prowess of jumping and fists, his stomach of
solitudes, his belly of burning iron…' Ginsberg's intentional listing
of sexual organs (and other body parts) provides a platform on
which he can expose his disrespectful interest in the unspoken body
part which he then turns into the written-spoken body part. Images
of gas stations and gymnasiums (where the homosocial activity of
sport supplies homoerotic imagery) come back in the love hymn
'Many Loves' in a much more openly explicit sexual way:

[…] the smooth mount of his rock buttocks, silken in
power, rounded in animal fucking and bodily nights over
nurses and schoolgirls,
O ass of long solitudes in stolen cars, and solitudes on
curbs, musing fist in cheek,
Ass of a thousand farewells, ass of youth, youth's lovers,
Ass of a thousand lonely craps in gas stations ass of great
painful secrecies of the years
O ass of mystery and night! Ass of gymnasiums and
muscular pants

ass of high school and masturbation ass of lone delight,
ass of mankind, so beautiful and hollow, dowry of Mind
and Angels, Ass of hero, Neal Cassady [...]
angel & greek & athlete & hero and brother and boy of
my dreams [...]

('Many Loves', 1956)

In 'Howl', the bodies are continually 'bickering with the echoes of
the soul, rocking and rolling in the midnight solitude-bench
dolmen-realms of love, dream of life a nightmare, bodies turned
to stone as heavy as the moon' and are 'confessing out the soul to
conform the rhythm of thought in his naked and endless head'.

Series of awakening shocks

The imagery of 'Howl' is like a roller coaster with alternating
hallucinations which seem to resemble drug-induced activities. His
approach to awaking shock techniques involve descriptions of
madness, emotional nakedness, sex, drugs and jazz and his
depictions of madness decorated 'with dreams, with drugs, with
waking nightmares' can be related to the more poetic hallucinations
of Rimbaud:

I have just swallowed a terrific mouthful of poison. –
Blessed, blessed, blessed the advice I was given!
– My guts are on fire. The power of the poison twists
my arms and legs, cripples me, drives me to the
ground. I die of thirst, I suffocate, I cannot cry. This is
Hell, eternal torment! See how the flames rise! I burn as
I ought to.

('A Season in Hell', 1873)

However, Ginsberg's list of 'poisons' is more accurate: 'the concrete void of insulin Metrazol electricity hydrotherapy psychotherapy occupational therapy pingpong table, resting briefly in catatonia'. The emotional upheavals and the series of shocks were required to awaken the young American from the dullness of the ordinary life. Unfortunately, even today's youth rely heavily on non-constructive activities, such as taking drugs, for their entertainment and this should reflect society's lack of responsibility to provide exciting cultural provision for its youth.

Body-harming and self-mutilation of Ginsberg's characters are described to have 'burned cigarette holes in their arms' or 'cut their wrists three times successively unsuccessfully' and this could be a clear reference to Rimbaud's hero in 'A Season in Hell' proving that Ginsberg was intrigued by the abject, non-beautiful nature of madness:

> My ancestors were Norsemen: they slashed their own bodies, drank their own blood. I'll slash my body all over, I'll tattoo myself, I want to be as ugly as a Mongol; you'll see, I'll scream in the streets. I want to go really mad with anger. Don't show me jewels; I'll get down on all fours and writhe on the carpet. I want my wealth stained all over with blood. I will never do any work.
>
> ('A Season in Hell', 1873)

Realisation that a new limit of individual expression had been reached:

> Madness was a topic never too far removed from Allen's mind. He still received an occasional letter from

his mother, who was lost in a world of paranoid fears. Two of Peter [Orlovsky]'s brothers, Nicholas and Julius, had been institutionalised in New York for mental disorders, and a third brother, Lafcadio, was reportedly having difficulties of his own. In April, Allen received word from Eugene that Carl Solomon, who had left his publishing job and was currently working as a *Good Humor* salesman in New York, had been hospitalized in Pilgrim State, the same hospital where Naomi [Ginsberg's mother] was a patient. The news was disturbing. 'What'll happen to Carl in time?', a concerned Ginsberg wondered.

(Schumacher, 1992, p196)

By dedicating 'Howl' to Carl Solomon, Ginsberg's genuine concern about Solomon's health is registered. The only way to fight madness and reach new limits of individual expression is by acceptance: accepting who you are and moving on. 'Don't hide the madness,' (Ginsberg, 'On Burroughs' Work', 1954) he writes two years earlier for William Burroughs. And in 'Howl', his mother-like concern is expressed in the lines 'ah Carl, while you are not safe, I am not safe'.

Ginsberg wanted to re-create the poetic form and in his own words 'to re-create syntax' which was similar to Rimbaud's wish to 'invent new flowers, new planets, new flesh, new languages'. Rimbaud went a step further than that:

> I invented colours of the vowels! A black, E White, I red, O blue, U green. I made rules for the form and movement of every consonant, and I boasted of inventing, with rhythms from within me, a kind of

poetry that all the senses, sooner or later, would recognise. And I alone would be its translator.

('A Season in Hell', 1873)

Ginsberg even felt the need to make sure that he can control time itself by writing about his friends 'who threw their watches off the roof to cast their ballot for Eternity outside of Time, & alarm clocks fell on their heads every day for the next decade'. Even if the ending hides some element of sarcasm, the sign of success is present. They tried to stop time, to ignore the fact that *Τα πάντα ρει* [everything flows], but failed. At least, they have experienced what it means to be original, individual and unique.

Epilogue

It is the belief in the art of poetry that has gone hand in hand with this man into his Golgotha, from that charnel house, similar in every way, to that of the Jews in the past war. But this is in our own country, our own fondest purlieus. We are blind and live our blind lives out in blindness. Poets are damned but they are not blind, they see with the eyes of the angels. This poet sees through and all around the horrors he partakes of in the very intimate details of his poem. He avoids nothing but experiences it to the hilt. He contains it. Claims it as his own – and, we believe, laughs at it and has the time and effrontery to love a fellow of his choice and record that love in a well-made poem.

Hold back the edges of your gowns, Ladies, we are going through hell.

(Williams in Ginsberg, 1956, Introduction)

The work of Allen Ginsberg speaks to all the senses. 'Howl' is a manifesto, a confession, a journey to an angry American man's world and back. Rimbaud's art was silenced after his 'A Season in Hell': 'I have to bury my imagination and my memories! What an end to a splendid career as an artist and storyteller!' Ginsberg was determined to have the lustful body present throughout his work with strong and powerful images of illicit erotic desire.

In part, because of that, the publication of *Howl and Other Poems* in 1956 would not pass without controversy. Within a year the volume faced the scrutiny of the courts. After an intense, and landmark, court battle during 1957 in which outstanding literary personalities defended 'Howl' as a significant comment on human experience, Judge Clayton W. Horn declared the work to be not obscene. In his decision he wrote: 'Life is not encased in one formula whereby everyone acts the same or conforms to a particular pattern. No two persons think alike. We are all made from the same mould, but in different patterns. Would there be any freedom of press or speech if one must reduce his vocabulary to vapid innocuous euphemism? An author should be real in treating his subject and be allowed to express his thoughts and ideas in his own words' (Feldman & Gartenberg, 1958, p164). And that is exactly what Ginsberg did. He continued to write about the human body until his final days with the optimism and disrespect of his youth:

> At 66 just learning how to take care of my body
> Wake cheerful 8 A.M. & write in a notebook
> rising from bed side naked leaving a naked boy asleep
> by the wall...
> put on white shirt white pants white sox...
> happy not yet to be a corpse.
>
> ('Autumn Leaves', 1992)

Remaining ever youthful in spirit, he used his art to document on paper, like Cavafy, the memories of his tempestuous life. And even if the tone becomes more serious closer to his end,

> Rainy night on Union Square, full moon.
> Want more poems? Wait till I'm dead.
> ('12AM Answering Mail', 1990)

his ability to shock/move remains unchanged,

> I can still see Neal's 23 year old corpse
> when I come in my hand.
> ('Approaching Seoul by Bus in Heavy Rain', 1992)

The 'naked body', Ginsberg's own body and the body of his work, will haunt the readers 'with the absolute heart of the poem of life butchered out of their own bodies good to eat a thousand years' ('Howl', 1956).

References

Breslin, Paul 1987 *The Psycho-Political Muse: American Poetry since the Fifties* (Chicago: University of Chicago Press)

Cavafy, Constantine 1961 *The Complete Poems of Cavafy* (London: Hogarth Press)

Feldman, Gene and Max Gartenberg (eds) 1958 *Protest: The Beat Generation and the Angry Young Men* (London: Souvenir Press)

Ginsberg, Allen 1956 *Howl and Other Poems* (San Francisco: City Lights)

Ginsberg, Allen 1996 *Selected Poems 1947-1995* (London: Penguin)

Kerouac, Jack 1957 *On the Road* (London: Penguin)

McClure, Michael 1982 *Scratching the Beat Surface* (San Francisco: North Point)

Rimbaud, Arthur 1975 *Poems* (London: David Campbell Publishers)

Schumacher, Michael 1992 *Dharma Lion: A Biography of Allen Ginsberg* (New York: St. Martin's Press)

Williams, William Carlos 1956 'Introduction' in *Howl and Other Poems* by Allen Ginsberg (San Francisco: City Lights)

Filming 'Howl'
A cinematic visualising of the text

Ronald Nameth
Interview

Simon Warner writes: The work of Ronald Nameth in the field of experimental cinema, in a career spanning more than 40 years, has earned him an international reputation. Born in Detroit but today based in Sweden, Nameth's activities as film-maker and promoter of the alternative film culture continue. In the 1960s, his ground-breaking incorporation of electronics and video to create 'visual music' established him as an important innovator. That aspiration, to test and extend the boundaries of the medium, persists.

In 1966, Nameth became closely involved with perhaps the most high profile multi-media event of an extraordinarily creative decade. Andy Warhol's *Exploding Plastic Inevitable*, a performance piece combining a dazzling array of artforms – visuals, sound and light, film, dance and rock music – had already attained a significant status in New York City.

When the production relocated to Chicago for a short residency, an opportunity arose to document the event. Nameth, by now based in that city, spent a week filming the show's performances at a club called Poor Richard's, eventually creating a widely acclaimed documentary that strove to capture the multiplicity of simultaneous features evident in the Warhol installation.

In his book *Expanded Cinema*, film writer and critic Gene Youngblood commented on his experience of the film of the *Exploding Plastic Inevitable*:

Andy Warhol's […] sensorium, the *Exploding Plastic Inevitable*, was, while it lasted, the most unique and effective discotheque environment prior to the Fillmore/Electric Circus era, and it is safe to say that the *EPI* has never been equalled. Similarly, Ronald Nameth's cinematic homage to the *EPI* stands as a paragon of excellence in the kinetic rock-show genre. Nameth […] managed to transform his film into something far more than a mere record of an event. Like Warhol's show, Nameth's *EPI* is an experience, not an idea. In fact, the ethos of the entire pop life-style seems to be synthesized in Nameth's dazzling kinesthetic masterpiece. Here, form and content are virtually synonymous, and there is no misunderstanding what we see […]

(1970, pp103)

Later technology – the emergence of digital formats, primarily – enabled Nameth to reproduce his multi-perspective recording of the installation and construct an environment in which the film could be experienced by the viewer on a series of screens at the same time, replicating the multi-sensory components of the original 'happening'.

I first encountered this remarkable presentation in Seattle at the Experience Music Project in spring 2005. Shortly afterwards, Nameth's documentary became part of a major touring exhibition celebrating the artistic explosion of the 1960s. 'Summer of Love: Art of the Psychedelic Era' was initially seen at Tate Liverpool and then Frankfurt and Vienna during late 2005 and early 2006.

It was at the Seattle screening of his documentary that Ronald

Nameth and I first discussed the possibility of creating a film which might respond to the poem 'Howl' and its 50th anniversary in October 2005. The plan to present a multi-disciplinary, commemorative event, *Howl for Now*, in the UK, provided a further catalyst to the film project which Nameth now hopes to develop.

In this interview, the film-maker discusses the impact of the Beats on his life as a teenage American, the emergence of an alternative film culture in the US of the Sixties, his involvement with the celebrated Warhol installation, and his thoughts on the creation of a film work which might reflect the spirit and energy of Allen Ginsberg's 'Howl'.

SW: How did the idea of a film linked to the 'Howl' anniversary emerge?

RN: It was really raised by our meeting in Seattle, when we were both attending the 2005 popular music conference, at the Experience Music Project. You mentioned your plans for a project called *Howl for Now*, to celebrate the 50th anniversary of the inaugural reading of Ginsberg's poem 'Howl'. Your description of this celebration brought up a lot of old, almost forgotten memories of my own experience of reading 'Howl' for the first time, in the late Fifties.

I was about 16 years old, living in Detroit, USA, and was in full rebellion. I had found in the writings of the Beats, a perfect mirror of my intense feelings at that time. They inspired me – primarily by the way they gave themselves the freedom to experience life intensely. Their search for themselves in 'the now' touched my own yearnings and I devoured everything I could read. As they threw themselves into their lives without reservation, their experiences opened the door in me to the possibility of a life lived fully.

Jack Kerouac and Allen Ginsberg had an especially strong impact on me. Their total abandonment to life was in stark contrast to the tied down, fear-filled life of middle-class society in the 1950s. Ginsberg's rage in the Fifties against numbing and dumbing of society was a perfect mirror of my own feelings. Later in the 1960s, Ginsberg's presence and his activities became a major element in the emerging alternative life style. It was incredible to see his clear stance and lack of fear in facing off to the establishment. His actions were a powerful message to many people.

SW: The Beats clearly impacted on you but how did you become involved in the creative arts yourself?

RN: As the Beat was transformed into the Hip, and the hippy and alternative movements expanded through the expanded consciousness of LSD, I became involved with making experimental films in Chicago. Working together in collaboration with other artists and musicians, many films were made as well as numerous trips to Mexico and San Francisco.

Some years later, I moved to the Champaign-Urbana area south of Chicago, into a community filled with creative people of all types. The new emerging technology of electronics was utilized to create visual music. Working all night at the university's Electronic Music Studio (after the electronic music composers had gone home to sleep), electronically-generated sounds were utilized to create moving forms with colour. These were then transferred to film.

This creative environment resulted in many collaborations with many creative people such as Steve Beck, the electronic synthesis engineer, Al Haung the Chinese T'ai Chi master and dance performer, composer Salvatore Martirano, poet M.C. Holloway,

John Cage, the musical inventor, the musician Michael Lytle, and many others.

SW: There was evidently a hot-house of artistic talent gathered in Chicago but, of course, Andy Warhol's links were principally with Manhattan. How did you come to connect with his *Exploding Plastic Inevitable* project?

RN: As I got involved in multi-media performances and light shows for music performances, I also created multiple-screen film environments – in particular for John Cage's first Musicircus and the Cage/Hiller HPSCHD music event in with 9,000 people participated. This work led to a contact with Andy Warhol's *Exploding Plastic Inevitable*, which is Warhol's most developed multi-screen multimedia environment.

To create the *EPI*, Warhol collaborated with some of the most creative people in their fields. In music, he collaborated with the Velvet Underground, which was composed of some of the most advanced rock musicians of the time, including Lou Reed, John Cale, Sterling Morrison, Mo Tucker, and the singer/actress Nico. Once adjusted to the initial sonic blast of the Velvet Underground, the listener could hear the undertones of R&B, improvisations of free jazz as well as the musical avant-garde and the mystical drone of LaMonte Young.

In November 1965, after completing several films in the dual-screen format, Warhol undertook to create his first multi-screened multimedia environment for the Expanded Cinema Festival at the Film-makers' Cinematheque in New York. Warhol then recruited the professional film editor, Danny Williams, who later became involved in the design of the light environment for the *EPI*.

It was in April 1966 that the first manifestation of the *Exploding*

Plastic Inevitable took place at the Dom, a former Polish dance hall turned club in New York, attracting many people and a great deal of publicity and media. The film-maker Barbara Rubin and poet Allen Ginsberg were among the personalities participating, as was the well-known news anchorman Walter Cronkite, who came by to see what was happening, as did Jackie Kennedy and much of New York's society. It became a major culture happening as news crews reported on the scene.

Warhol said of this time: 'We all knew something revolutionary was happening. We just felt it. Things could not look this strange and new without some barrier being broken'.

SW: So Warhol's show was clearly making waves and attracting high profile interest. How did the film project itself get off the ground?

RN: Warhol's production then came to Chicago for a residency at Poor Richard's. During one week of performances of the *EPI* in June, 1966, I worked every night filming, to make a comprehensive recording of the event. Because the *EPI* environment is a multiple screen projection environment, the film utilised multiple level super-impositions of imagery that sometimes reaches a depth of five layers. The film works extensively with the experience of time through its changing rhythms of motion. The film material was the only extensive motion picture document of the *EPI*. This film material was to create several versions in order to present as complete a document as possible – one version was for single screen projection while another version was for a 4-screen video installation that re-creates the spatial experience and environment of the *EPI*. A photographic exhibition was also created.

SW: What sort of reaction was generated by the *Exploding Plastic Inevitable?*

RN: There are various critical and academic responses worth re-visiting, I think. Kate Butlers, a journalist wrote about the *EPI*, saying: 'The *Exploding Plastic Inevitable*, generated during the 1960s, has often been cited as the pioneering multimedia experience. Audiences were bombarded with floor to ceiling projections of Warhol films such as *Vinyl*. At centre stage, the Velvet Underground were transported with Warhol-directed lighting effects. Images filled the show, that were disturbing and abrasive as Lou Reed's songs. Collaboration between artists and musicians had never before, or since, proved so influential despite its short life span'.

Later, Branden W. Joseph, the art historian at the University of California, wrote: 'The *Exploding Plastic Inevitable* remains as the strongest and most developed example of intermedia art. Although (other) productions […] have since achieved greater technical dexterity on a visual plane, no one has yet managed to communicate a guiding spirit through the complex form as well as Warhol and the Underground'.

SW: How would you describe your own aesthetic approach to documenting this phenomenon?

RN: In filming the *EPI*, my intention was not to create a documentary, but instead to create a light/sound experience that would allow the viewer to re-experience, to some extent the actual event, without any verbal description. Since *EPI* was a multiple-screen, multi-sensory experience, and since I had only one screen (the film) I chose to use multiple levels of super-imposed imagery together, to come as close to the original experience as was possible.

There were also a number of technical limitations that would affect the making of the film. First, no artificial light would be used, as this would have destroyed the environment of lights and projected imagery. Yet, at the same time, film in the Sixties was not particularly light-sensitive. To solve this problem, I operated the camera at 1/3 the normal speed, thus allowing more light to reach the film surface. Normally, when film is projected at 8 frames a second, instead of the normal 24 frames a second, it results in a choppy, speeded-up effect.

To avoid this, each frame of the recorded film was put into a device known as a contact printer, and each frame was then printed three times, thus creating 24 frames per second. This resulted in a kind of freeze-effect, in which normal motion is slightly frozen in a short space of time. This effect transformed 'normal' reality into a kind of other-worldly place – a slight warp of time and space. This time/space warp was then edited and super-imposed into a depth of five levels of imagery.

The cinematic style of *EPI*, and in most of my films is quite impressionistic – there seems a strong sense of atmosphere over form, suggestion over narrative, the implicit over the explicit. Atmosphere, suggestion, non-narrative, and the implied – all these are forms which allow one to go beyond the logical, rational mind, into realms that cannot be accurately presented with words.

When the technology of DVD discs became available, it was then possible to expand the original recordings of the *EPI* into a four-screen video environment, so that a space with multiple-screens could be created to provide a more intense experience of the original event.

SW: You have intentions to work on a film commemorating 'Howl' and its 50th anniversary. Could you describe how you might approach this project?

RN: For the planned production of the film to celebrate 'Howl''s 50th anniversary, the intention is to present a multi-faceted expression of the poem through the live performance *Howl for Now*. By presenting 'Howl' as a multi-faceted experience, via music, drama and monologue, the intention is to touch upon Ginsberg's original experiences and mirror the reality he projected in his original poem.

As with *EPI*, the *Howl for Now* production will work with multi-media and with a multi-disciplinary subject – spoken word, drama, music, imagery. Like *EPI*, it is intended to be in a single-screen form, as well as a multiple-screen video installation environment. Each of these forms will present 'Howl' in a way that is appropriate for that particular structure.

A lot of contemplation has gone into how to approach this work. There is a clear sense of what needs to be filmed, and what needs to be captured. At the same time, it is impossible to plan entirely – as reality always provides surprises. So, much reflection and contemplation will also be given while in the editing process. It is here that the creative process continues, and one finds the threads that will create the reality of the film and the form for the multiple-screen video installation environment.

Considerable thought has already been given to the form of the single-screen version. Several recordings are planned. The first will be of the live event, which sets the tone and mood for the dramatic aspect of the work, as the participants and performers will be in the space with a live audience.

In a second recording session, I plan to physically move into the space on-stage and work directly in the performance space so that I can interact directly with the performers. They will thus be able to perform directly into the eye of the camera.

A third recording session is envisioned, in which the performers are moved from the stage, into the outside world – into streets and alleyways, again performing directly for the camera.

Additional imagery will be gathered and edited into these recordings. This imagery will be indicative of the period of the Fifties and mirror the depth of experience in 'Howl'.

In film and video recording process, one works sequentially, first to gather together all the various elements necessary to the piece. One could perhaps compare it to the cooking of a meal. First, one must have all the necessary ingredients. When everything necessary is available; then comes the work of mixing everything. With traditional editing, conscious decisions are made to structure the material. One can also involve the use of chance operations (such as those of Burroughs or of Cage), so that the rational, logical, ego-mind is set aside in this process and thus allow unexpected combinations and juxtapositions to occur.

The single-screen version is most often shown in the context of a film projection environment, which means that people sit in chairs and watch the screen from beginning to end. (That is, if they don't fall asleep of boredom or leave in exasperation or desperation!) So, this aspect has to be taken into consideration.

The multiple-screen video installation environment offers a very different environment compared to traditional single-screen film viewing, since the viewer is free to walk freely in the space, and choose their own experience of how they wish to experience the space. This is similar to the act of viewing a painting in a gallery, or simply moving about in one's daily life. Here, there is no suspension of reality, as in the traditional film presentation. Instead, one is free in time and space to move and select one's own experience of the work.

In an environment with multiple screens, the use of a traditional visual language is not vital or necessary – one is free to allow juxtapositions of image, form and movement that would not work in a single-screen situation. Here, chance has a greater opportunity to play, and to allow the viewer to become the participant in the experience of the space.

With the possibility of creating two very different experiences of Ginsberg's poem as presented in *Howl for Now*, the intention is to provide a multi-faceted, in-depth and varied experience that will reveal the depth of Ginsberg's vision, and mirror the reality he experienced.

Reference

Youngblood, Gene 1970 *Expanded Cinema* (originally published 1970, New York: P.Dutton & Co, Introduction by Buckminster Fuller) at <http://www.vasulka.org/Kitchen/ PDF_ExpandedCinema/ExpandedCinema.html> [Accessed September 5th, 2005]

The visual arts and 'Howl'

Painters and poets in the American 1950s

Michael Anderson

The atmosphere of possibility, the creative energy infusing the art world on both of America's coasts during the later 1940s and through the 1950s, cannot have failed to touch Allen Ginsberg and his creative circle. This was a time when the predominance of the European tradition, stretching back more than half a millennium to the heart of the Renaissance, was at last challenged by the painters and sculptors of the US as dynamic new movements: first Abstract Expressionism, and its potent offshoot Action Painting, to be followed by the precursors and practitioners of Pop Art, ensured that the seat of power, both aesthetically and commercially, truly shifted from Paris and the Old World to New York and California.

Yet for Ginsberg, as his poetic voice took mature shape in the early Fifties, there were lessons still to be learnt from older traditions, too, and, as he gathered diverse influences and sources – from Blake to Buddha and beyond – and sought to forge a break with his earlier formalism, the affect of a grandmaster of the Post-Impressionist school on his artistic development was far from insignificant. There are certainly signs that the work of painter Paul Cézanne played an important part in fuelling the creative momentum that would ultimately produce a poem like 'Howl' in 1955. What inspiration did an eminent French painter, dead by 1906, bring to the poet's musings during this period?

It was in 1948, the year after Ginsberg's visionary encounter with the English mystic William Blake, that the American poet initially became drawn to Cézanne. Enrolling on a course on modern art that autumn he 'became entranced […] about the considerable impact […] Cézanne had made on modern art'. He was 'particularly interested in Cézanne's experiments in perception – specifically his use of perspective, form and colour modulation to alter his own and his viewer's appreciation of the phenomenal world' (Portugés, 1995, p142).

Ginsberg was fascinated by a particular structural aspect of Cézanne's paintings: he was intrigued by a sensation that two colours, juxtaposed, could give. The poet referred to this as 'a sudden shift, a flashing that you see in Cézanne's canvases' (Miles, 1990, p97) and he would eventually make direct reference to this in 'Howl', Part 1: 'Who dreamt and made incarnate gaps in Time & Space through images juxtaposed…jumping with sensation of Pater Omnipotens Aeterna Deus'. The Latin phrase – 'All-powerful Father, Eternal God', in translation – was drawn from a 1904 letter from Cézanne to Emile Bernard (Portugés, 1995, p147). 'A major element of Ginsberg's compositional technique was to be an attempt to find the equivalent in words of Cézanne's gaps, a choice of words that would create a gap between them, "which the mind would fill with the sensation of existence"'(Miles, 1990, p97) Miles adds that Ginsberg's favourite example was a phrase from 'Howl': 'hydrogen jukebox' (*ibid*).

Cézanne's was a structural device: in constructing his paintings he was searching for an architecture of form within nature. He painted his subjects – for instance, *Mont Sainte-Victoire* – repeatedly, not to capture a likeness, but as an unchanging form to which he could variously submit his intentions to reveal intrinsic geometric structures. The 'gap' moved Ginsberg because through it he could see how form, text and meaning could be present by implication. Ginsberg wanted to 'show his readers supernatural phenomena […]

Blake had accomplished such miracles in his poetry; Cézanne had created a similar effect in his paintings. How could Ginsberg create that 'flash' in his work? In 1954-55, Ginsberg discovered the answers to these questions while writing 'Howl'. He had learnt through various techniques to translate insights gained in his Blake and Cézanne studies into his own art form' (Portugés, 1995, p148). Anton Ehrenzweig proclaimed that 'Motifs preserve their fertility only if their connection with the final result remains obscure' (2000, p52). The gap that Ginsberg was moved to pursue in his own work rules out single or precise interpretations in 'Howl'. Instead, and more richly, the gap provides for reflection and inference.

Ginsberg's search for fresh modes of personal expression at this time was far from a solo odyssey. The decade after the Second World War's conclusion was a period when artists, musicians and writers made bids for intellectual and emotional freedom and developed the simultaneous courage to exercise their power and will to direct and celebrate their individual uniqueness. Jack Kerouac's stream of consciousness literature, Charlie Parker's extraordinary extensions of the jazz code and John Cage's musical experimentations with indeterminancy are just some of the examples of the ethos of artistic invention which informed the era.

In the field of the visual arts what came to be defined as 'Abstract Expressionism' grew somewhat inevitably as a defiant commitment to questioning expectations and adding reason and experiment to more commonly expected values. It materialised during a period that would include the spectre of McCarthyism and other attacks on the freedom of individuals and institutions, together with the projection of grand strategies of imperialistic states. It came after the anguish of a war in Europe and Japan terminated by the woeful flight of the *Enola Gay* and its terrible cargo, bringing a period of history to a close and opening the age of dawning realisation: the world had undergone cataclysmic changes and needed new modes of expression to depict the aftermath. Whether in painting, where fresh visions took shape, or in literature, where poetry and the novel undermined pre-war certainties, artists at the edge tested the parameters of possibility.

Abstract Expressionism is still a descriptor that defines an art that is an *American* art. There had been in Europe, before the Second World War, a powerful tradition of abstract art, a trend that survived into the ensuing decades. But the transitions that occurred in painting in the States during the 1940s and 1950s, as expressed through that thread of abstraction which became known as 'Action Painting', defined an American experience that was quite specific and separated from that of the European one. Although there was a growth in abstract art in the UK, for example, during these years, these developments did not provide a real parallel. British painting articulated a consummate understanding of its roots and sources but the stunning realisation in the American artists was that subject and object could be removed from the works. Freeing themselves from rules and historical precedents, artists were primarily engaged in laying the physical bulk of paint on to a resistant support material such as canvas. In brief, that summed up this new and ground-breaking aesthetic.

After those long centuries in which Europe had held pride of place in the artistic pantheon, suddenly the US began to make great and challenging strides, producing work in which the sub-conscious, chance and automatism directed the material quality, displacement of colour, and tone, the textures, surfaces, the sweep of pigments and media. Art critic Harold Rosenberg declared 'The work, the act, translates the psychologically given into the intentional, into a "world" – and thus transcends it' (in Harrison & Wood, 1996, p582). Works were often very large, large enough to make demands of whatever space it occupied and of all those who passed by it. Paint, loosely and vigorously applied, shaped works that would not direct the gaze towards something seen or known but addressed the aspects of their own making and circumstances. They were about themselves; they contained their own histories. Rosenberg described the paintings as evidence of the gestures of the artist when 'at a certain moment the canvas began to appear to one American painter after another as an arena in which to act – rather than a space in which to reproduce, redesign, analyse or express an object, actual or imagined' (*ibid*, p581).

Existentialism, essentially a European import via the French wave of philosopher novelists, Sartre and Camus, was making its impact on American painting and writing. It was reflected in the Abstract Expressionists of the US as it was, a little later, in the novels of Kerouac and the verse of other Beat poets. They were controversial: they celebrated spontaneity and proposed non-conformity. Their art, on canvas or on the page, was a revelation implicit in a gestural engagement when the artist defines a moment of her/his time.

The titles of the artworks rarely relayed a sense of subject of reference. Consider Robert Motherwell's extensive series 'Elegy to the Spanish Republic'. Begun in 1948 (Fineberg, 2000, p70) and numbering over 170 canvases, some as long as 12 feet, it is not impossible to read the series as emblematic. Yet they did not emerge from a specific response to the Spanish Civil War. They were made after the re-discovery of a small collage the artist had made some years earlier that was unrelated to that Iberian conflict. At the point he stumbled upon this potentially insignificant work, the artist had been moved by Federico García Lorca's poem 'Lament for Ignacio Sánchez Mejías' which, with poetry, passion, and violence, tells of the death of the bullfighter. Lorca's poetic refrain line 'at five in the afternoon', drives, punctuates and gives tempo to the poem. It presented to Motherwell an opportunity for a graphic equivalent in *At Five in the Afternoon*, as his own motif, repeated across his collage, performed a similar function. These commanding, mainly black and white works, stand amongst the very major works of the 20th Century. Fineberg remarks on these: 'In this painting the austerity of the monochrome palette and regimentation of the composition into regular bars and ovals provide a dramatic foil for the spontaneous emotive elements, such as the loose gestural brushwork, the paint drips, and the artist's rebellion against the self-imposed compositional order of alternating bars and ovals. The resistance to order embodied in the personal eccentricities of the work stands for resistance to order on wider fronts – psychologically, politically and culturally' (2000, p70).

In 1952, David Smith, leading American sculptor of his generation, declared that 'present day, contemporary America is producing masterpieces – a virile, aggressive increasing number of painters and sculptors not before produced here' (in Harrison & Wood, 1996, p579). There was a dialogue between artists as there was between members of other literary and artistic communities including the Beat Generation writers. During the Forties and Fifties, artist members of the New York School, including Jackson Pollock, Willem de Kooning, Mark Rothko, Franz Kline, and Motherwell met regularly at the Cedar Tavern, Greenwich Village. It was also a meeting place for Ginsberg, Kerouac, and other members of the Beat community. The artists were aligned with the Beat poets and had a clear knowledge of both contemporary art and literature. They were not unaware of the art that preceded them in America and Europe; they knew what had gone before. Like many of the Beat poets, making art owed less to conventional narrative but instead fervently pursued that freedom that would allow them to explore their own intentions, devices and constructions. Neither group was inclined, certainly initially, to consider, much less address, perceptions of a 'public'. David Smith's position was synchronous with the group when, in 1952 in a speech given at Deerfield, Massachusetts, he declared that the artist makes art 'for himself first, for the opinion of other artists next' (in Harrison & Wood, 1996, p578). Smith and Motherwell were particularly eloquent and through writings and lectures lucidly communicated the nature and circumstances of art practice.

As with the Beats, the Abstract Expressionists mediated their experiences through their materials and by extending the conventions of their media. They believed in their freedom and the principle of consequence as a basis for understanding and heightening experience of the human condition. Apart from much yawningly inevitable, ubiquitous, peripheral civic art in the form of public murals, monuments and the face of coinage, achievements and civic preferences are not commemorated in abstract art nor are they within Beat culture. As the Beat poets engaged with personal realities, were moved and affected by contemporary culture and ideologies that cut across class and institutions, so the visual arts, on the same course, addressed and re-defined what art might be and how its direction could be effected.

Poetry and art had become procedures for exploring visual and literary space. They were locating and positioning themselves to propose new realities. They were generally perceived as anarchic, and subversive, unwilling to identify for themselves what constitutes acceptable political, professional and social behaviour. The many photographs of the Beat Generation and associates including tableaux, documented gatherings and intimate groupings provides no evidence to the contrary as they celebrated their cause and their coming together.

In the early 1950s the first stirrings of what would eventually be dubbed Pop Art was running close behind abstract painting. The careers of the new movement's leading American exponents – Robert Rauschenberg, Jasper Johns, Claes Oldenburg and Edward Kienholz – were already underway in the early Fifties. Rauschenberg and Johns extended their work in painting to combine three dimensional objects, too, and more adventurous experiments in collaboration. At Black Mountain College, the progressive school in North Carolina, they collaborated with composer John Cage, choreographer Merce Cunningham, pianist David Tudor, composer Lou Harrison, inventor and architect Buckminster Fuller and other artists drawn into the cross-media developments, including Motherwell and Kline. They pursued work that combined art with dance, music and theatre. In this respect their importance extended the public consciousness that art could extend and enrich consciousness.

Drawing its themes from mass culture, such as advertising, movies, popular literature, music and packaging, Pop Art was an inevitable reaction to the prevailing Abstract Expressionist philosophy. It rejected the dominance of the purely visual, contemplative object as it was imbued with the particularities of its execution. Pop Art had the feature of declaring a populist, accessible, non-elitist culture while echoing the deconstruction of form and structure in other art forms including film, jazz, and Beat poetry, as well. Linking conceptually with the position of Dadaist pioneer Marcel Duchamp, the major precursors of Pop Art, Rauschenberg and Johns, were also informed by the ideas of John Cage. Together, they incorporated notions of populist art, its distribution, and its extension into music, theatre and dance performance. The new work was informed not just by mass-cultural imagery but also by the means of production. Silkscreen printing, photo-lithography and other photo-mechanical processes were included and were often dependant upon collaboration between artist and technician.

Rauschenberg who had given classes at Black Mountain College in 1945 and 1951 (Fineberg, 2000, p70) continued to visit and work there on visual and performance pieces until the early 1960s. Rauschenberg recalled that in the 1952 work *Theater Piece #1*, Cunningham improvised a dance around and through the audience while Cage read a lecture on Meister Eckhart, M. C. Richards recited from a ladder, Tudor played piano and Rauschenberg himself projected slides of his paintings while playing old records on a hand-wound Victrola (see Ruckhaberle et al, 1980, p22).

In 1965, Donald Judd announced that 'half or more of the best new work of the last few years has been neither painting nor sculpture' (Harrison, 1991, p37). He identified West Coast artists including Kenneth Price and Edward Kienholz, and New York's Claes Oldenberg and remarked that their works resembled sculpture more than painting though it 'was nearer to painting' (*ibid*). Kienholz was involved with the California Beat Generation opening the Now Gallery in Los Angeles in 1956 to present the work of avant-garde artists. Kienholz produced installations, sculpture and assemblages that included found objects and the waste ephemera of contemporary society. They were painted and made on a human scale. For example, *The Portable War Memorial*, a full-sized environmental reconstruction (at least 30 feet across) of the renowned photograph of US Marines raising the Stars and Stripes on Mount Suribachi in the Pacific island of Iwo Jima, over the centre-hole of an outdoor café table as if it were a parasol. A Coke machine stands at the end of this bizarre tableau.

Kienholz occupied ground opposed to mainstream culture who, like the Beats and countercultural intellectuals were drawn to

Eastern religious traditions including Buddhism. His installations and sculptures operated as a critique of contemporary culture, injustice and moral degradation. He brought together copious and disparate found objects and materials to create richly visual yet deeply disturbing imagery. The paraphernalia and apparel of everyday situations were combined to provide situations in which the everyday – hypocrisy, falsehood, institutional abandonment, brutality – were made explicit and presented as side shows. They provided a critical appraisal of contemporary society, and a commentary on the political climate. Kienholz, Johns and Rauschenberg were central to the activities and discourses that combined to expand the nature and locations of art practice. Discourse was generative at the level where the action was taking place including independent galleries, meeting rooms, clubs and bars.

Larry Rivers was also a significant artist and bridge between the visual arts and Beat literature. He was, says Fineberg, 'the outstanding painterly realist to emerge in New York in the Fifties' (2000, p165). Rivers was a jazz saxophonist until 1945, and a long-term close friend of poet Frank O'Hara, who shared associations with the Beats. The painter also collaborated with another poet, Kenneth Koch, on a collection of picture-poems in 1959. Twenty years after that, Koch, with Ginsberg, produced a recording, 'Popeye and William Blake Fight to the Death' (1981), an improvised rhyming contest before an audience. O'Hara, commenting on Rivers, observed that his main interest was in the immediate situation: what held as true for one day may not always be the same. Rivers' paintings and sculptures included Camel cigarette packets, Dutch cigar boxes carrying a reproduction of Rembrandt's *Syndics of the Drapery Guild*. He had no desire to present his images as socially significant, saying, in 1963: 'I think what

I choose to look at is based primarily what out there will allow me to use what's in my bag of tricks' (in Russell & Gablik, 1969, p103). In this, he was not, of course, dissociating himself from others. The empirical isolating, re-ordering and developing of content and structure happen in art and poetry and are a very real concern, not just for Rivers. Much later, in 1972, a Rivers painting *The Athlete's Dream* (1956) would adorn the cover of the Penguin Modern Classics edition of Kerouac's *On the Road*.

As we have seen, the dominance of the Abstract Expressionist project was plainly American. Yet Pop Art, for all its Stateside pizzazz and appropriation of imagery from the US urban and commercial landscape, also had a British wing which actually took flight before its American counterpart. Richard Hamilton and Eduardo Paolozzi were largely credited for initiating Pop Art in the UK, particularly through the 1956 exhibition 'This Is Tomorrow' at the Whitechapel Gallery, London. Yet Hamilton, Paolozzi and other UK colleagues, quicker out of the starting blocks, would see their American equivalents – including Andy Warhol and Roy Lichtenstein – become even bigger international stars.

However, it is through another American Pop painter that the eminent critic Robert Hughes draws a line between that art stream and the Beat writers. James Rosenquist, whose massive billboards for the ascending advertising industry in the Fifties inspired him to make them into his own artworks, produced images that were 'a painted equivalent to the casual-portentous, side-of-the-mouth prophetic tone that had come to American poetry […] through Allen Ginsberg and the Beat writers under the threat of the atom bomb' (Hughes, 1980, p353). The artist himself made reference to this connection: 'When I was working in Times Square and painting signboards, the workmen joked around and said that the super-centre of the atomic target was around Canal Street and Broadway.

That's where the rockets were aimed from Russia…The Beat people, like Kerouac and Robert Frank, Dick Bellamy, Ginsberg and Corso, their first sensibility was of [the bomb] being used immediately and they were hit by the idea of it, were shocked and sort of threatened' (quoted in ibid, p354).

The Pop artists in responding to a popular, contemporary culture of consumer design, film and TV media 'aimed to extend and to focus art's sociological penetration and to revise the interests of high art by reference to the imagery of popular culture. Their measure of modernity was taken from the world of distribution' (Harrison, 1991, p16). The wry practitioners of Pop Art and the Beat poets injected heavy doses of irony and re-presented the everyday encounter as an opportunity for a range of interpretations and responses. Print and photo-mechanical processes enabled the inclusion of news photographs, reproductions of old masters and commercial graphics onto canvases and assemblages. But we have to just hold back a bit on the temptation to describe these people as torch-carrying radicals driven by a socio-cultural agenda: they came from different backgrounds and with intentions that varied considerably. Yet there is no debating the impact they had on their own era and the period that followed. Art and literature stepped out of the shadow of the academy and embraced the world of the street, its language and its iconography.

References

Ehrenzweig, Anton 2000 *The Hidden Order of Art* (London: Weidenfeld & Nicholson)

Fineberg, Jonathan 2000 *Art Since 1940: Strategies of Being* (London: Laurence King)

Harrison, Charles and Paul Wood (eds) 1996 *Art in Theory 1900-1990* (Oxford: Blackwell)

Harrison, Charles 1991 *Essays on Art & Language* (Oxford: Blackwell)

Hughes, Robert 1980 *The Shock of the New: Art and the Century of Change* (London: BBC)

Miles, Barry 1990 *Allen Ginsberg A Biography* (London: Viking)

Portugés, Paul 1995 'Allen Ginsberg's Paul Cézanne and the Pater Omnipotens Aeterna Deus' in *On the Poetry of Allen Ginsberg*, edited by Lewis Hyde (Ann Arbor: University of Michigan Press)

Russell, John and Suzi Gablik (eds) 1969 'Symposium on Mass Culture and the Artist', Statement read to the International Association of Plastic Arts by Larry Rivers at the Museum of Modern Art, New York October 1963, in *Pop Art Redefined* (London: Thames & Hudson)

Ruckhaberle, Dieter, Elke Hartmann and Monika Hoffmann (eds) 1980 *Robert Rauschenberg 1950-80* (Berlin: Staatliche Kunsthalle)

Terenzio, Stephanie (ed) 1999 *Collected Writings of Robert Motherwell* (Berkeley: University of California Press)

Ginsberg, Allen and Kenneth Koch 1981 'Popeye and William Blake Fight to the Death' from the poetry album *The World Record* featuring Various Artists, St Mark's Poetry Project

A soundtrack to 'Howl'
First thought, best thought

Bill Nelson
Interview

Simon Warner writes: Bill Nelson has been navigating those choppy waters between rock and jazz, contemporary music and the avant-garde, for almost four decades, never fully immersing himself in one style, always pressing on to find new means of expressing his musical voice. His career, documented in a recorded repertoire stretching to some 50 released CDs, has embraced the blues and jazz, progressive and art rock, glam and the new wave, music for film and theatre, ambient soundscapes and drum'n' bass.

From the late 1960s he strove to combine elements of popular music and the visual arts – he was both guitarist of reputation and a graduate of a British art school, sharing those characteristics with English rock stars from John Lennon to Keith Richards, Eric Clapton to Pete Townshend – seeking a synergy between his song-writing and the influences of those potent 20th Century artistic impulses – from Futurism to Dada, Pop Art to US comic books – he had absorbed as a student.

Attracting the early attention of John Peel, the UK's most important popular music broadcaster, Nelson's recordings speedily gained national airplay and, when his band Be Bop Deluxe were signed by EMI, their sequence of four critically and commercially acclaimed albums revealed a distinctive marriage of inventive rock music and stylish album sleeve imagery, underlining their leader's keen interest in both sound *and* vision.

After enduring the pleasures and pains that accompany the life of the guitar hero – he was corroded rather than encouraged by the adulation and expectation, scarred by the rigors of the nascent US stadium circuit – he dissolved Be Bop Deluxe, formed a band with new wave nuances called Red Noise, and then settled into a long period of making music as solo composer, as label owner – his own Cocteau Records ran in the 1980s – and collaborator, working with artists as diverse as Japan's Yellow Magic Orchestra, Channel Light Vessel and the American avant gardist Harold Budd.

The catalyst for the interview that follows is a project in preparation, to compose a soundtrack to a planned film, based on 'Howl', by the eminent US film-maker Ronald Nameth. Here Nelson describes his attraction to the literature of the Beat Generation, how he approaches the process of composition, and offers some clues as to how he might deal with the challenge of creating a score to accompany Ginsberg's most celebrated verse work.

SW: You have taken an interest in the Beat writers for many years. How was your interest in these novelists and poets sparked?

BN: I was an art student in the mid 1960s, a period of positively optimistic cultural discovery, despite the fears generated by the Cold War and Vietnam. English art schools provided the perfect environment for creative exploration back then. I remember that, during my first year there, I was at Wakefield Art School in West Yorkshire, the older students were of the generation that venerated the Beats. I was straight out of secondary modern school and fairly naive about such things but I recognised that these more seasoned students fitted the popular image of 'the beatnik'.

The senior students appeared as strong, independent characters to me, some of them colourful to the point of eccentricity. They often would stop what they were doing and recite strange poetry out loud and in a very dramatic, exclamatory fashion, oblivious to what anyone else might think of their behaviour. I was somewhat in awe of them, being little more than a shy schoolboy. Within a few weeks, however, I got to know some of them personally and picked up on their various influences and passions.

My own generation were mods, out of rock'n'roll and moving towards the cusp of psychedelia. Bit by bit, we found our way into the emerging 'underground' music and art scene. I remember ordering, from a little Wakefield newsagent's shop, copies of *International Times*, the independently published countercultural newspaper, which regularly featured articles about Allen Ginsberg and William Burroughs. The publication was hardly known outside of certain circles at that time, at least in Wakefield, and reading it was like being let in on some exotic secret. I can recall reportage, in the publication, about the big poetry reading held at the Royal Albert Hall in London in 1965. The event featured Allen Ginsberg, Gregory Corso and Lawrence Ferlinghetti (amongst others) and created some interest and controversy in the mainstream media. I could only imagine, from the article and a couple of accompanying photos, how exciting it must have been…but it kindled my curiosity even further.

William Burroughs had attended this event, although he hadn't given a live reading, and it was his *Naked Lunch* novel that became my first Beat Generation purchase. Of course, I was both intrigued and shocked by the book. It was perhaps the most radical thing I'd ever read, but I thought that the cut-up technique brought a strange beauty to material that might otherwise, at that time, have seemed sordid and prurient. It was the subject of much discussion amongst my fellow art students.

As the British counterculture grew and consolidated itself, I was able to discover more about its roots, which were, to some degree it seemed, entrenched in American soil. I'd had a strong interest in American pop culture for some time, starting out with super-hero comic books when I was very young, and popular films and music of course. At art school, I came across books in the library that referenced American 'underground' cinema and avant-garde music. I'd been a jazz fan for a while, being a young guitar player, but suddenly read about people such as John Cage and Harry Partch. Their creative ideas inspired me and I could see how there was a 'connected-ness' to the world glimpsed in the pages of *International Times*. Yoko Ono was another discovery and the Fluxus group. None of this was exactly Beat Generation but, in some ways, it felt like a complementary force. I could sense kindred spirits. The American film experiments of Stan Brakhage, Jonas Mekas, Ron Rice, Ken Jacobs, Kenneth Anger, Jack Smith, Maya Deren, Harry Smith and others seemed connected to the Beats in some way too, though, for me, seeing anything other than stills in obscure art publications proved difficult.

In more recent years, I've revisited all of these artistic territories, as one often does when one reaches a certain age. Naturally, my understanding has deepened with the passing years but I still find fresh inspiration from the writers, musicians and artists of that era.

SW: In what ways did they inspire or affect you?

BN: It's not always easy to pinpoint exactly why some things make such an impact on one's life. It goes deeper than 'liking' something, I suppose. There's definitely a feeling of kinship, of finding that one is not alone. A confirmation of sensibilities? There was also, for me at that time, a sense of being opened up to wider possibilities, an exciting, new-found freedom of expression. It was almost as if one had been given permission to dream in colour, instead of just black and white.

SW: How do you feel the influence of the Beats may have fed into your musical and wider creative work?

BN: In general terms, the influence is part of an entire era that opened up many of my generation to our creative potential. It's a historical 'passing of the torch' that moves from one artist to another. But, in more specific terms, Jack Kerouac's 'first thought, best thought' dictum is something I've held to for some time now. I'm a firm believer in allowing the sub-concious a space within the work, a space in which it can make itself felt. I have to acknowledge the way that the Beat Generation's exploration of mysticism, particularly the Eastern variety, laid the foundations for my own investigations into that territory, even though some of it came 'second hand' via the hippy route pioneered by Timothy Leary and Ken Kesey's Merry Pranksters. Not that I ever was brave enough to dabble with psychedelic drugs…I decided I had more than enough visions, dreams and nightmares to keep me awake at night without poking around in my even darker attic of demons!

SW: Are you touched by the spirit? Or are you affected by the form? Do you owe any kind of lyrical debt, for example, to the kind of techniques that Jack Kerouac, Allen Ginsberg, William Burroughs and other members of that literary community devised?

BN: Both, but perhaps the underlying spirit of it is more important to me, although quite a few rock musicians have tapped into Burroughs' (and, more accurately, Brion Gysin's) cut-up techniques. I've used variants of this in my lyric writing of the Seventies and early Eighties. Methods of introducing chance into the work.

Of course, John Cage devised various similar but different

techniques to produce purely musical or sonic results, techniques aimed at bypassing the conscious mind of the artist. A different philosophical basis to Burroughs' approach, perhaps, but essentially a way of working with what appears to be chance. During my career with my 1970s era band Be Bop Deluxe, I recorded a piece called 'Futurist Manifesto'. It was, quite obviously, named after the document issued by the Italian Futurists at the beginning of the 20th Century but the technique I used to create the lyrics owes a big debt to Burroughs and Gysin, rather than to Marinetti, Balla and Russolo.

I picked up a copy of *Country Life* magazine that was lying around in the studio where the band were recording the album *Drastic Plastic* and, from an article chosen by simply opening the magazine at random, took the first word from the first line, the second from the second line, and so on, right through the article, until I had enough words to fit the piece. It wasn't a cut up or a 'fold in' as Burroughs and Gysin would think of it, but it was allied with their approach. It was also surprising what this technique threw up. There *were* some conscious adjustments on my part afterwards though, just to get it to flow more interestingly in certain places, but not too many. I then made three tape recordings of the resultant text, speaking the words, rather than singing them.

These recordings were then played back on three tape recorders, deliberately out of sync with each other. This produced random audio juxtapositions of the text. The three tapes were then dubbed, whilst in this out of sync fashion, onto the main multitrack machine on which I'd previously created a music bed, again, using Cage's and Burroughs' concepts as inspiration to create the sounds. The finished piece had an otherwordly quality that might have escaped if I'd have used more orthodox means. The strangest thing was that it all appeared to have 'meaning'. It resonated with an authenticity that suggested a conscious impulse or 'hidden mind' was operating behind the work.

In more recent years, I've actually written songs dealing with various Beat inspired ideas and also a song loosely around Jack Kerouac's celebration of the road journey as a kind of mythical quest. My solo album *After The Satellite Sings* provides the easiest reference to this kind of material, particularly tracks such as 'Streamliner', 'Flipside' and 'Memory Babe'.

SW: Have you drawn on literature in a wider sense when you come to compose? Are there characters or episodes, are there narratives or dramas on the printed page that have actually prompted you to pen particular musical or lyrical responses?

BN: I don't really use literature 'literally' in that respect. I generally don't write about characters from books or adapt fictional scenarios, although there have been the odd exceptions. I'm more often inspired by an author's honesty or willingness to open himself up to the experiences of his life, than any desire to take hold of his characters or subject matter and use it within my own work. I feel — and this is purely my personal approach here, no criticism intended of all those artists who adopt or appropriate fictional scenarios and characters — that I'm only properly equipped to comment on my *own* life and so my songs are, in the main, autobiographical, experiential, diary-like things. They are often cloaked in symbolism or encoded in some way but essentially, they are my life and dreams, hopes and fears, captured in sounds and words and pictures. Snapshots of a life. The music and form can become quite complex and multi-layered but, the essence is simple and single-pointed. Perhaps selfish and self-obsessive sometimes too, I cheerfully admit. But this is what constitutes my 'prima materia', the stuff from which I attempt to transmute my philosopher's stone.

So...aside from considerations of pure aesthetics, I use my work to try to reveal myself to myself, it's an attempt to figure out some quite fundamental philosophical problems, often by examining the most ordinary and banal aspects of my existence. In this respect, Kerouac's work has shown me that this is nothing to be afraid of. Ginsberg's too. His writing is as open and as direct as possible. Its honesty escapes the shackles of its beauty and stands naked and unashamed.

Every single person has a complex and emotional story to tell, or a song to sing. It's ultimately deserving of the mystical wonder that Kerouac saw in so many things. Something to be revered and respected. Of course, whilst life is enriched by the pursuit of such ideals, they ultimately don't save us from ourselves or our demons. If anything, this approach brings those demons into sharper focus. It's a difficult confrontation. Seeing them face to face can be a dangerous thing. I think Jack Kerouac's direct vision was a double-edged sword for him. It's the same for all artists, to one degree or another. Part of the price we pay for the privilege of *seeing*, perhaps? Lots of available theories about this, Freudian, Jungian, Reichian, etc, etc...It gets over-romanticised too. 'The ever popular tortured artist effect' as someone once put it.

This is another interesting thing about the Beats' work for me: it explores the nature of the artist, the role of the imagination, the nature of *vision*. It seems perfectly natural that Ginsberg and Kerouac should find solace and inspiration in Buddhism – Tibetan in Allen's case, Zen in Jack's – and that Burroughs should be drawn to occultism. In their own ways, these were deeply *spiritual* men, the holy trinity of the Beats. Gary Snyder was, perhaps, the most 'authentic' in this respect though. At least initially.

SW: What are your feelings about a poem like 'Howl'? When did you initially encounter it?

BN: I can't remember *exactly* when I first read 'Howl'. It could have been the late Sixties. I certainly remember reading *about* it before I actually read the work itself. Even back then, its opening lines were often quoted in alternative publications. When I actually got to read it, what initially came across was the sheer energy of the piece, the torrent of passion, anger and beauty that leapt from the page. For all its epic length, it was tight and focused, for all its sense of outrage and horror, it was elegant and aesthetically seductive, an undeniable masterpiece and a turning point for poetry in general at that time. God knows how it must have appeared to the uninitiated when it was first published. It's almost impossible to imagine the shock and controversy it would have caused back then, so much have public sensibilities changed in the intervening years. But it was, without a doubt, a *revolutionary* work. It's also a work that continues to resonate, that rewards re-investigation. I think you could easily say, 'timeless' despite the clearly defined cultural signifiers of that period.

SW: What approaches might you take if you compose a musical work which references a literary work in some fashion?

BN: The approach is generally dictated by two things, the work itself and my personal reaction to it. It's impossible to always 'get' the author's intention in its purest sense, one can only work from one's response to the writing, but the piece's history along with received knowledge about its author's inspiration are bound to colour one's responses to some degree. Essentially though, it's a subjective exercise. It's best if I'm moved in some way, emotionally, aesthetically, by the work. The intellectual content may or may not interest or connect with me, but if I can somehow 'feel' the core of the piece, then this isn't such an essential consideration.

With poetry, the *spoken* word is key to much of the music's composition. Metre, inflection, timing, tonality all contribute to the musical experience of a poem. Different readers will bring their own persona to bear on this, in much the same way that different musicians will interpret an individual composer's work. It's a little like jazz or improvised music in this respect. Until the actual performance, it's difficult to predict the final result.

I like to include hidden layers of meaning, reference points to time and place, the environment surrounding the creation of the poem, little signifiers that might be picked up by those who have studied the piece in more depth than the casual listener. At the same time, there needs to be an emotional, visceral charge that connects with and illuminates the work for even the most casual listener. It's tricky and can be hit and miss. You can spend a very long time trying out various avenues of possibility before hitting on the most appropriate approach. Then again, you can simply just 'go for it'. First thought, best thought!

SW: How might you attempt to make a musical response to a piece like the Ginsberg poem?

BN: Read and re-read the piece, make rough notes as to possible instrumentation and tonality. Research the circumstances surrounding the poem's birth, the music of the time, Ginsberg's own musical tastes, the political/social impulses that inform the poem's content. Try to see how much of this can be used as inspiration but not neccesarily portrayed in a literal sense. It's a form of abstraction, a reduction of things to essentials without losing the plot, you might say.

It would also be good to use recordings from the era, music, sounds, news broadcasts, as background 'interference'. These could even be manipulated live by others at the appropriate points in the piece.

Ideally, there should be an opportunity to compose the music directly to a recording of the spoken word. The most effective way would be to record the poem being spoken by the actual person chosen to read it at the eventual public performance...then use their 'guide' voice as a template to create the music and assemble the sounds. My own preference would be to use a pre-recorded music bed with just a few live improvisations, rather than attempt a totally live, real-time musical score. There could certainly be elements of live improvisation though. Whilst the eventual public reading might vary to some degree (compared to the guide vocal) the recorded music would offer an appropriately structured response and also a 'map' of sorts for the reader to work with. I find that, no matter what plans one makes as to method, technique, etc, the end result is always something else, something that emerges through the moment by moment response to the materials at hand and the prevailing winds of the imagination. It's simply a matter of throwing oneself overboard and trusting that the muse will guide one to the shore. Sometimes, too much thinking and planning can close off more interesting and rewarding avenues of exploration. It should be a joyful adventure, not a scientific exercise or surgical dissection.

Musical responses to 'Howl'

Compositional approaches to the text

Michael Spencer and the
Howl for Now composers

Simon Warner writes: The performance *Howl for Now* was conceived as one that would draw centrally on the power of the spoken word but would also represent a multi-disciplinary response to a significant piece of poetry. While the verse work was always going to provide the anchor of this commemorative event, discussions took place from the outset about the incorporation of music into the occasion. What that musical score might be was left quite open as we all felt that the performance we constructed should be as much about contemporary responses to the 1955 poem as a celebration of the first reading and its original historical context.

Michael Spencer, Lecturer in Composition at the University of Leeds, took the role of musical director though he has acted throughout rather more as a catalyst than a controlling force to a group of young composers who were invited to produce pieces for *Howl for Now*. The composers are principally postgraduate students in the University of Leeds School of Music who have worked alongside Spencer in the last two years. They have produced work in a variety of idioms – electronic and electro-acoustic, orchestral and chamber, jazz, rock and dance – so their compositional ideas and processes run the gamut of contemporary music-making.

In this chapter we gather a series of loosely constructed commentaries and responses, involving the eight composers engaged in this musical project, including Spencer himself. The section aims to cast light on a number of creative processes: how a literary text might have a relationship with a musical work or score; how a composer approaches the problem of devising new music to reflect that text or distil some of its essence; and how composers working half a century on from this significant poem's emergence can connect its ideas and attitudes with the early 21st Century landscape.

Adam Fergler

Stanzas of Gibberish (Nothing in Black or White Makes Sense)
[Clarinet; trumpet; piano; percussion; electric guitar; bass guitar; theremin; electronics]

The first part of Allen Ginsberg's three part protest poem 'Howl' bombards the reader with image upon image in a single and relentless stream of consciousness; each of the vivid depictions rolls seamlessly into the next, the solitary full-stop being reserved for the very end. The effect of this on the reader is one that can only be described as brain-shattering: a seemingly endless outpouring of ideas and views presented in an almost incomprehensible fashion. It takes many readings to even begin to understand the use of language and the run-on sentences.

After reading 'Howl' for the first and the umpteenth time my thoughts were something along the lines of 'Oh hell…' It became immediately apparent to me that I would be unable to present Ginsberg's ideas through music in a programmatic sense, nor would I be able to bounce any ideas of my own off the poem in an attempt to create a stimulus for composition for fear of losing all of my ideas (and possibly my mind) in a thick literary soup. Instead, I decided to re-present the poem, to impart it through my own artistic medium, filtered through my own reaction to – and interpretation of – the text.

Stanzas of Gibberish (Nothing in Black and White Makes Sense) is the result: a three part musical structure in which the main, central section is designed as the musical equivalent of a stream of consciousness, where ideas disappear as readily as they occur, eliding with each other as they come and go. This is prefaced by a short section in which piano harmonics coupled with a sharp bass drum attack tear open the sound world that ordinarily is only allowed to exist inside my head and release it into the 'real' world. America's national anthem, 'The Star-Spangled Banner', then ensues in a heavily contorted form marked, 'Without pride: with anger and a lack of faith'. In the final section of the piece 'The Star-Spangled Banner' returns as various fragments, at various speeds and in various (implied) keys. This in itself makes quite a racket, nevertheless, the entire ensemble is simultaneously recorded, played back at a slower speed, and digitally manipulated to make as much 'dirty' noise as is possible. This cacophony subsides to leave a baron, desolate sound world that delivers us into silence, the bass clarinet's rapid cycling of pitches referencing Charles Ives' *The Unanswered Question* leading our ears back to our ordinary lives with an air of uncertainty. (This final section reminds me of the line 'Go fuck yourself with your atom bomb' from another of Ginsberg's poems, 'America').

The use of material from other pieces should not be perceived as my lack of originality, but rather as a way of expressing Ginsberg's apparent contempt towards the establishment: America's national anthem is made to sound as corrupt as the government of its country; The 'Trumpet Voluntary' (used as pitch derivation system for the main part of the piece) is manipulated so that its tonality is never clear (the tune is put into the minor mode

121

while the bass-line is dropped a major third, but remains in the major mode) and what should stand for boldness, readiness for battle and pride now intones uncertainty, doubt and instability. The material from *The Unanswered Question* has the same 'eternal' function here as it does in Ives' work, though here it also questions the integrity of which the two quotations stand for.

The title *Stanzas of Gibberish* is intended as an observation of a gut reaction to 'Howl' following first exposure and is taken from part one of the poem. The subtitle, *Nothing in Black and White Makes Sense*, alludes to the fact that the written word can only ever be a monochrome reduction of a Technicolor imagination, as, for that matter, is the printed musical score. (The similarity between the name Ginsberg and that of the delightful drink Guinness creates the possibility of a pun which is not entirely intentional. Some years ago Guinness was advertised using the slogan 'nothing in black and white makes sense'.)

Roddy Hawkins

Put on Hold

[Clarinet; trumpet; piano; percussion; electric guitar; bass guitar; theremin; electronics]

In recent weeks, I was reading 'Howl' quite a bit. A few things struck me. Firstly, there is the way in which lines run into one another, confusing all sense of metaphor and placing a rather hazy drug-infused imagery around the frame of my imagination. For instance, a line can equally refer to the line before and to the line after, and it completely screwed with my sense of time and direction as I tried to navigate my way through imagery which I found hard to relate to.

The energy of the poem I found easy to relate to. Exactly what it is I find hard to describe, but it almost certainly involves the anti-establishment overtones, something with which I sympathise (albeit in very different ways and for some different reasons). And by establishment I refer to the way things are now in the Western world. Who cares for art? Who cares for public policy that helps the many and not big business? Who really runs the world? The leaders of G8? There are feelings of utter despair and uselessness that came across to me in the poem. All the hysteria and madness I view as a symptom of 'the way things are'. It is 'the way things are' that interests me.

It is worth mentioning the use of the only full stop at the end of the text and the unusual line breaks which give this tumbling forward momentum, and yet the direction of imagery can be the reverse. This leads to a sort of panic when reading it. As I was being rushed forwards by the energy I was thinking, 'Hang on a minute! I didn't quite catch that last bit…Oh bollocks, now I'm somewhere else'. I wanted to somehow capture that energy in musical terms yet also capture the despair at the stagnation of our position. I suppose it is arguable that the two are so tied up in one another that there's is little point trying to deconstruct the whole thing.

So there I was, phoning my bank, to find out how much money I didn't have, and they were charging me 30p a minute to listen to piped music interrupted every now and then by a friendly person telling me that if I just waited for a few minutes an advisor would be with me shortly. I gave up, I couldn't care, so I started listening to the bollocks they play down the phone and the ways in which the voice messages interrupt the music and then the music re-starts not where it left off, but as if it has carried on all the time during which I've been told how important and valued I am as a customer. What if I missed the bass fill in 'I Want You'? Music is mistreated so badly in so many ways; I can kind of see why Adorno went a little mad.

I decided that I would compose some filler music, where the most distinct and memorable character of the whole piece would be the voice message. This idea neatly fitted with my interpretation of the poem. It allowed me to plan an overall structure where: firstly the process of shortening each section creates an instant panic and energy/momentum and secondly that the repetition/control of material in each section allows the monotony and despair at this situation to exist.

I don't think I can separate these two strands of my thinking in the way I have tried to do. That said, there is a balance between pre-compositional planning, and then a manipulation of material within certain set structures. It is as if I have a series of frames for painting. Each one gets smaller and smaller, and they are all made up before any 'material' is created. I have set myself such boundaries to limit the endless possibilities that could occur within the frames. If I can control the time, energy flow, of the overall plan, then my primary concern of distorting the audience's perceptions of time, is addressed (not necessarily achieved), and it is then down to what happens within this framework to see whether or not a distortion of time is successful.

Vicky Burrett
The Ghostly Clothes of Jazz
[Clarinet; trumpet; piano; djembe]

The opening of the poem conveyed a sense of mysticism and lament. I made a direct translation of this mood into the opening bars of my composition. The monotonous and chime-like piano part is rich with ambiguous harmonies, and the clarinet's low trills add colour and effect to the atmosphere. I purposefully alternated the time signature in these first eight bars to reiterate the fact that the rhythmic pulse of the poem is continually changing. Ginsberg jumps from one image to another with great spontaneity and pace, which is so characteristic of the whole poem.

The emotional content of the poem also alternates, and does so without much warning. I have tried to capture this energy in the 5/8 sections, with the chromatically descending piano sequence which is reinforced by the djembe. Strong jazz influences play a large role throughout the piece and this is first hinted at here within the exploding 5/8 section in the clarinet part.

I have also tried to depict the anger and aggression (and at times, madness) which is characteristic in the first part of the poem when Ginsberg describes the different minds of his generation — the recurring 5/8 sections relate back to these emotional outbursts of 'madness'. After this sudden interruption, the mood from the beginning of the piece returns but now with a more mystical and lazy-jazz approach to it (the previous 5/8 section acted as an introduction/preparation to this).

The return of the main motif is now played by the clarinet but this time, expands its range by over an octave in comparison to the trumpet's previous statement of the motif. In many ways, this relates to the poem's emotional expansion and the development of the events which Ginsberg is portraying. The piano's block chords contrast greatly by playing the prominent motif with an alternate harmonic accompaniment; again, developing the already stated motif.

The 5/8 section soon returns, and is as sudden an interruption as before. This time, however, the djembe is the driving force behind the section and maintains the steady 5/8 swung beat. I have tried to relate this section to the second part of the poem, which comes across with more accusation regarding times within modern-day society. Triple time meters have been added amongst the 5/8 bars to portray the lack of fluidity with regard to the rhythmical pulse of the poem.

I found the last part of the poem the most emotional where Ginsberg is writing with so much power, longing and compassion; a reaffirmation of the heart. The last section of the piece therefore relates directly to the compassionate, dramatic and powerful emotions within Ginsberg's writing. Using the extremities of the piano's keyboard and the dissonant harmonies produced by the trumpet and clarinet, the pulse of the piece returns to the original tempo to create a very powerful and effective sound. In responding to Ginsberg's 'Howl' I have broken many of the boundaries I had as a composer, much as he broke away from both literary traditions as well as the constraint of freely voicing opinions.

Adam Longbottom

Dreams and Drugs and Walking Nightmares

[Electronics]

A piece exploring the subjects of nightmares, suicidal tendencies and darkness of the mind, creating an environment of 'supernatural ecstasy'. Using music and drama *Dreams and Drugs and Walking Nightmares* focuses upon the death-like images evoked by the poem 'Howl'.

The music for this piece is wholly electronic, combining several electro-acoustic techniques, concentrating especially on time stretching and pitch bending processes. It includes sound effects, vocal samples and synthesised music.

Other thoughts: Having a background in film music composition, I treated the images conjured up in my mind whilst reading the poem as the material that I was to compose for. Intending to use lights and stage performers to enhance the piece, these images also helped with the overall visual premise.

I want the piece to be much more than a musical work. I want it to be an experience for the audience in which they would really feel the subject matter. The use of performers, lights and staging is therefore critical.

Musically, the piece starts with abstract noises intended to be the 'walking nightmares' made flesh (something visually apparent on stage too). It then gradually grows into a more conventional musical form using a constant beat, harmony and melody.

Eleri Pound

the madman bum and angel beat in time
[Clarinet; trumpet; piano; percussion; acoustic guitar; bass guitar; theremin]

I have never written a piece in response to text before without actually setting the text itself for a voice part so the first issue to solve was how I was going to create a piece that relates to the poem.

On reading the poem the first thing that jumped out at me was the rolling lines, endless words relating to each other in one extended sentence. The reader is led through a stream of consciousness, occasionally getting stuck on an idea before moving quickly through the next few different images. It was quite easy just to read through, being rushed along almost unaware of what the meaning of the text was except for phrases every so often that struck a chord.

Much of my research in composition revolves around using mathematics to derive pitch and rhythmic series and to determine the structure of pieces, mostly using the Fibonacci series. I decided this composition would give me the opportunity to try out another system that I had been interested in implementing; coding theory. I decided I would like to emulate the seemingly endless sentence of the poem by using a constant percussion part in the composition.

Taking parts of the text I coded it first into the numbers 1–24 according to the alphabet and then reduced it to ternary form, that is 0, 1 and 2. I then assigned these numbers to different drum strokes on the djembe, which speaks the coded text throughout the first section of the piece. The other instruments also derive from this coded text although they generally use a more detailed generational process. These instruments pick up on certain parts of the djembe text and elaborate on it by using the more sophisticated language.

The second section moves from the djembe to the tubular bells allowing the percussion line to speak in a more detailed voice. The tubular bells invoke the image of the 'hopeless cathedral' bells where the other instruments are calling out their prayers of desperation for salvation. The pitched instruments still continue to elaborate on the images of the previous section but are also offering their cries and prayers to the tubular bells.

The sound-world I have used has obviously been affected by the pitch series I have created but I was also aware in the back of my mind the desire to reference certain sound-worlds that I associated with this poem. For example, muted trumpet is used to invoke the jazz element of the period, and I have used the constantly changing time signatures to emulate the changing rhythm of natural speech.

Jon Barnard and David Gammie

Pingpong of the Abyss
[Clarinet; trumpet; piano; drum kit; electric guitar; bass guitar; theremin; electronics]

David Gammie writes: We engaged predominantly with the emotive qualities of the poem, considering how it made us feel from one initial reading. We'd both read it before but were not ultra-familiar with it and so we wanted to just see how it made us react on the spot. We discussed and agreed that it had a real feeling of assault; the non-stop, non-punctuated verses creating a relentless sense-bashing and we knew that we wanted our music to reflect this in some way. Considering the period and the Beat scene, we wanted to incorporate some sort of jazz element, which can be heard mainly through the chord-structures. We picked out rhythms from certain lines of text and used them as templates for passages in the clarinet and trumpet and the drum-kit at the opening and close of the composition is designed to hammer away in the same style as the unremitting verses of the text. During individual and separate readings, Jon and I selected a few pieces of text that really stood out and there were two lines in particular that we both had highlighted:

'Pingpong of the abyss'
and
'Hydrogen jukebox'

We took the first as a title and incorporated ideas from both into our piece. Passages reflect each other, a phrase played on clarinet is then 'batted back' by the trumpet, and this was designed directly from the idea of ping-pong. 'Pingpong of the abyss' seems like another, more descriptive title, capturing the themes we locked into. We used a recording of an actual game (of ping-pong) to create a percussion track to add texture and intrigue to the music. Using computer software we were able to sync the hits to precise points in a bar, allowing us to create organic drumbeats from sounds that were kept in the order they played. We also recorded the atmospheric sounds of a busy pub so that we could combine it with the sampled ping-pong and create a textural accompaniment to the live instruments and drums.

We wanted to create an assault in the music that would begin and end the piece, so we agreed that we would use a kind of rock-group sound, incorporating the orchestral instruments. The theremin in particular, really worked with the guitar to create a riotous bombardment of sound. Although we did not want the middle section to lose momentum, we wanted to provide a break that would work to accentuate the following return to the noise. We agreed that a certain level of dissonance was necessary to capture the feel of 'Howl' and this really came through in the guitar and bass parts in the intro. We also wanted the time signature to be unpredictable so used a 'rocky' 4/4 but wrote patterns of 7 or 9 to create unpredictability and a rhythm closer to the poem.

Michael Spencer

Ayahuasca Haze

[Clarinet; trumpet; piano; percussion; electric guitar; bass guitar; theremin]

Ayahuasca Haze is a short response to Ginsberg's 'Howl' (Part 1). It is not an attempt to literally translate the imagery, text or rhythm into music; rather, it focuses on capturing the energies of the poem in a relatively abstract way. There are certain textures that occur in the work that have been suggested by the poem such as the insistent use of percussion beaters inside the piano at the opening. Also, there is the use of 'triggers' to create particular energies – for example, the tam-tam attacks in section A trigger sharp-edged gestures in the trumpet and piano. This triggering technique seems to function as an oblique reference to the 'sparking' of imagery in the poem which rapidly moves from universities to New York, through walking nightmares to Brooklyn and on to the 'endless ride from Battery to holy Bronx'. What is particularly striking about Ginsberg's style is the effortlessness with which he moves from one astonishing image to another and this in many ways relates to my compositional approach over the last ten years which has focussed on finding ways to segue extremely varied musical types perhaps gestural, timbrel or in terms of pitch material.

Structurally, there are several 'controlled' regular sections that break down (cf. the poem) – other structures replace these and also collapse creating a gradual overlapping of texture (for example, the electric bass part from section C).

Ayahuasca Haze is in five sections: an opening section at $\varepsilon = 56$ 'with the utmost raw energy'; A ($\varepsilon = 78$) which consists of a dialogue of fairly complex rhythmic material between the clarinet and trumpet over a backdrop of rippling piano and amplified distortion; B – the three futile attempts at reconciliation of the whole ensemble; C, where there is the introduction of extended techniques in the wind and brass and hammer-on ostinato patterns in the guitars that gradually break down through the section leading into an overlapping bridge section to D; D – which, while more stable in overall textural terms, contains fluctuations on the microlevel (the use of slate in the percussion and the sustained vibrato notes on the guitars); and E ($\varepsilon = 56$) which combines some of the elements from the previous sections with a haunting bowed vibraphone line.

The bubbling clarinet part in section D is probably, in retrospect, an attempt to capture the 'moto perpetuo' energy of the poem – the player has very few places to breathe! It is an augmented, magnified version of the ululating guitar and theremin parts which is then ornamented and decorated with trills, flutter-tonguing, tremelandi, and quarter-tone inflections.

One way that the poem directly 'appears' in *Ayahuasca Haze* is in the expression markings which are for the performers' benefit and are not to be spoken or revealed to the audience other than through the performance itself. Having scanned the poem for 'stand-out' lines, I collated many more than I required for the five minutes of the piece and then selected several; sometimes before the music had been written, sometimes after. The most obvious example would be 'Three times successively, unsuccessfully' which is a direction for the triple attempt of the ensemble to play a quarter-tone inflected chord together, one of the few times that there is anything approaching rhythmic unison in the work.

Of course, no composer particularly likes discussing their work verbally or in written form, and most would argue that the music should be listened to rather than dissected.

Notes on contributors

Michael Anderson, Senior Lecturer in Contemporary Art Practice at the University of Leeds in the UK, was formerly Head of the School of Art and Design at Bretton Hall. He currently teaches art, focusing particularly on fusions between painting and digital media. Current and recent exhibitions and presentations include 'Collaborations' (in Miami), 'Pro-forma Pause' (Kansas City), 'Uncertain Objects' (Milan), 'Digital Prints' (Vermont), 'Bali Hai' (Hong Kong) and a contribution to 'Hibrida' (Brno, Czech Republic). A keen collaborator he is involved in projects in New York and Malta. He recently worked with organist Louise Marsh to produce a CD of organ music with accompanying illustrated book (published by OXRECS) as a visual investigation of *La Nativité du Seigneur*, nine meditations for church organ by Olivier Messiaén.

David Meltzer is a Bay Area resident who teaches in the Humanities and Poetics programmes at the New College of California. He began his literary career during the Beat heyday in San Francisco, reading poetry to jazz accompaniment in the Jazz Cellar. He has published numerous volumes of poetry, a series of novels, and collections of commentary and criticism, including *Reading Jazz* (Mercury House, 1996), *Writing Jazz* (Mercury House, 1999) and *San Francisco Beat: Talking with the Poets* (City Lights, 2001). In 1968 his rock band Serpent Power released their eponymous album. Collections of his verse have been anthologised by Black Sparrow

Press and his most recent poetic work, *Beat Thing*, was published by La Almeda Press in 2004. A new volume gathering his poetry is currently in preparation by Viking.

Ronald Nameth has been utilising photography, film and video since the early 1960s to create works for both single-screen presentations and multiple-screen video installation environments. He has collaborated extensively with many artists, writers, musicians, and poets including musical inventor John Cage, Pop artist Andy Warhol, photographer Aaron Siskind, artist William Wegman, poet M.C. Holloway, composer Salvatore Martirano, photographer Art Sinsabaugh, artists Rob Sweere, Ramon Lamarca, Linda Gustavson, Gunilla Bade, and many others in making these works. He was also one of the first wave of artists in the early Sixties to utilise the emerging technology of electronics and video to create visual music. His works have been broadcast, screened and exhibited around the world.

Bill Nelson is a guitarist, songwriter and composer who has brought his creative talents to a wide range of recording, cinematic, theatrical and art projects. Between 1974 and 1977, with his band Be Bop Deluxe, he made a series of commercially and critically well-received albums – *Axe Victim*, *Futurama*, *Sunburst Finish* and *Drastic Plastic*. In the 1980s and 1990s he continued to produce a sequence of eclectic and inventive albums under his own name. In 2004, he issued an autobiographical volume based on his own creative odyssey, *Diary of a Hyperdreamer* (Pomona, 2004). His latest recordings *Rosewood Volumes 1 & 2* (2005) provide a showcase for recent acoustic guitar instrumentals.

George Rodosthenous was awarded a PhD in Musical Composition in 2001 at the School of Music, University of Leeds, UK, and is now Lecturer in Music Theatre and Programme Manager for the BA in Theatre and Performance at the School of Performance and Cultural Industries, University of Leeds. His main research interests are 'the body in performance', 'conducting the body', 'theatre as voyeurism' and 'the interfaces of music, text and movement'. He has composed music for over 30 theatre productions, as well as television series and short films. As Artistic Director of the Theatre Company, Altitude North, he has directed music theatre pieces in UK, Canada, Greece and Cyprus. He is currently co-writing the book *Theatre Music Narrative: Non-Verbal Trends In Performance since the 1990s*.

Michael Spencer is currently Lecturer in Composition and Aesthetics at Leeds University, UK. His music has been performed at the Huddersfield Contemporary Music Festival (he has been twice short-listed for the Young Composers' Competition in 2000 and 2003), Instal 2002 (Glasgow), Maxis 2003 Festival (Leeds), at the Darmstadt Ferienkurse (2004), by Ensemble SurPlus in Freiburg and Stuttgart, and extensively at Glasgow, Manchester and Leeds universities. Current work in progress includes *The Lynx Arc* (for solo improvising alto sax, 12 players, Electronics and Video Projection) – part of a 7-work cycle in collaboration with Scottish artist Lesley Anne Derks and an ongoing cycle exploring the notion of fragmentation in music called *Message from Aiwass. The Eemis Stane –Homage to K.S. Sorabji* is due out on a CD collection of new piano music recorded by Aleks Szram (fonorum label).

Steven Taylor is Associate Professor at the Jack Kerouac School of Disembodied Poetics at Naropa University in Boulder, Colorado, and Director of the Naropa Audio Archive. He holds a PhD in music from Brown University and is a member of the seminal underground rock band the Fugs. In 2003, he published *False Prophet: Field Notes from the Punk Underground* (Wesleyan University Press), a memoir/ethnography accounting five years in the life of a guitarist with the New York hardcore band False Prophets.

Simon Warner teaches popular music at the University of Leeds in the UK. A former rock journalist – he was a reviewer with the *Guardian* from 1992-95 – he is also Director of PopuLUs, the university's Centre for the Study of the World's Popular Musics. His publications include *Rockspeak: The Language of Rock and Pop* (Blandford, 1996) and a chapter in *Remembering Woodstock* (Ashgate, 2004). His next book *Text and Drugs and Rock'n'Roll: The Beats and Rock from Kerouac and Ginsberg to Dylan and Cobain* will appear through Continuum Press of New York. In addition, he edits the electronic publication *Chapter&Verse, A Journal of Popular Music and Literature Studies* (www.popmatters.com/chapter).

Howl for Now composers

Jon Barnard, Vicky Burrett, Adam Fergler, David Gammie, Roddy Hawkins, Adam Longbottom and Eleri Pound, along with Michael Spencer, are members of FOCAM (Forum of Composers and Musicians), the Leeds University School of Music's contemporary and new music collective. (www.focam.co.uk/forum)

Note: Examples of musical works featured in the *Howl for Now* performance can be accessed via the internet. For more details visit the website www.leeds.ac.uk/music/research/PopuLUs

Useful Links

The Allen Ginsberg Trust has a website where you can explore published as well as never-before-published text, photos, handwritten documents and audio and video materials representing Allen's life-work. The website is intended to continually reveal the intelligence and beauty of Allen Ginsberg's aim of increasing consciousness on the planet.
www.allenginsberg.org

PopuLUs, the Centre for the Study of the World's Popular Musics, is one of the research centres based at the University of Leeds School of Music. The centre takes a scholarly interest in popular music styles of all kinds around the globe.
www.leeds.ac.uk/music/research/PopuLUs

Chapter&Verse – A Journal of Popular Music and Literature Studies. An electronic journal, published under the auspices of PopuLUs, and edited by Simon Warner. Launched in 2004, this bi-annual edition considers those areas where popular music and literary forms overlap.
www.popmatters.com/chapter

Bill Nelson – *Dreamsville* is a website devoted to music, art and creativity. It has been built as a safe haven and a source of information for all those who have an interest in Bill Nelson's life and work and its related subjects.
www.billnelson.com

Jack Kerouac School of Disembodied Poetics at Naropa University was founded in 1974 by Allen Ginsberg and Anne Waldman.
www.naropa.edu/writingandpoetics/

Index

Route

For full details of Route's book catalogue, including the innovative byteback books, plus MP3 audio files, interviews and features please visit:

www.route-online.com